Innovative Pricing Strategies to Increase Profits

Innovative Pricing Strategies to Increase Profits

Daniel Marburger

First published in 2012 by
Business Expert Press, LLC
222 East 46th Street, New York, NY 10017
www.businessexpertpress.com

ISBN-13: 978-1-60649-381-6 (paperback)

ISBN-13: 978-1-60649-382-3 (e-book)

DOI 10.4128/9781606493823

Business Expert Press Economics and Finance collection

Collection ISSN: 2163-761X (print)
Collection ISSN: 2163-7628 (electronic)

Cover design by Jonathan Pennell
Interior design by Exeter Premedia Services Private Ltd.,
Chennai, India

First edition: 2012

10 9 8 7 6 5 4 3 2 1

Printed in the United States of America.

Abstract

The practice of setting a single price that all buyers pay is slowly becoming a thing of the past. Today's marketplace requires firms to develop innovative pricing strategies to remain competitive. Is it better to bundle goods or price them separately? What type of online auction will generate the most revenue? The purpose of this book is to use microeconomic theory to determine which pricing strategies will succeed, and under what conditions.

Keywords

Price discrimination, bundling, price skimming, price penetration, online auctions, English auction, Dutch auction, first-price sealed bid auction, second-price sealed bid auction, price elasticity, consumer surplus, two-part tariffs, quantity discounts, quality choices, tying, peak-load pricing, dynamic pricing, e-commerce, pricing, Robinson-Patman Act, winner's curse, reference price, private value auction, common value auction

Contents

List of Cases/Firms/Products

Chapter 2

1. Netflix Qwikster

Chapter 3

1. National Association for Convenience Stores
2. Toyota Prius

Chapter 5

1. University of Alabama athletic department
2. Johns Hopkins University
3. Airline Deregulation Act
4. Priceline and Hotwire
5. American Airlines and Delta Airlines
6. Marriott Corporation

Chapter 6

1. Disney World
2. Quicken
3. DirecTV
4. McDonald's Corporation
5. IBM versus United States
6. United States versus Paramount Pictures, Inc.
7. United States versus Loew's, Inc.
8. Apple iPhone
9. Dell Computers
10. Gillette Fusion Power
11. Walmart Corporation
12. Costco and Sam's Club
13. Microsoft Windows Live One Care
14. Universal Studios Portofino Bay Hotel

PART I

If You Could Choose any Price, What Would it be? Fundamentals for the Single Price Firm

CHAPTER 1

Economics and the Business Manager

What is Economics all About?

Mention the word "economist" and one conjures up a vision of an academic who scours over macroeconomic data and utilizes sophisticated statistical techniques to make forecasts. Indeed, many economists do just that. But some people may be surprised to learn that economics is a social science, not a business science. Like psychology, sociology, anthropology, and the other social sciences, economics studies human behavior. That includes consumer behavior, firm behavior, and the behavior of markets.

In its simplest form, economics is a study of how human beings behave when they cannot be at two places at the same time. If you take a job that requires extensive travel, the income and opportunities for advancement come at the expense of spending time at home with the spouse and children. No matter how badly you may want the career opportunity and still spend quality time at home with the family, you cannot have both. You're going to have to choose. The idea that we cannot have all the things we want is called *scarcity*, and it plays a role in every decision we make; not just financial decisions, but nonfinancial ones as well. Do you want to stay up late to watch the ballgame on TV if it means you won't get a full night's sleep? Do you want to read the financial pages on the Internet or watch your son pitch in the Little League game? Scarcity forces us to lay out our opportunities, prioritize our activities, and choose accordingly.

Consumers do the same with their incomes. They cannot spend the same money twice, so scarcity (in the form of a finite income) forces them to determine what they can afford, prioritize the possibilities, and decide what to purchase and what to do without. The latter point, *"what to do without,"* is relevant to both spending decisions and the uses of one's time. As long as you cannot be at two places at once, whatever you choose implies the alternatives you must forego. Likewise, because you cannot spend the same money twice, each purchase decision you make implies those you cannot make. Economists refer to this as **opportunity cost**. In understanding human behavior, most economists will acknowledge that opportunity cost is the most critical concept in decision-making.

Let's begin with a simple example of the role of opportunity cost in business: negotiating the price of a new car. Most consumers dread negotiating with the salesperson. They assume the salesperson has superior information and will take advantage of them. In fact, the salesperson and customer are negotiating to find a mutually beneficial price; the final act of negotiating is more an act of cooperation than confrontation.

When a consumer decides to buy a new car, he recognizes that monthly car payments supplant the purchase of other goods and services he values. Moreover, the better the car, the higher the price, and the greater the opportunity cost. Opportunity cost helps him determine how much he is willing to spend on a car, and what types of vehicles fall within that price range. Once he decides on a vehicle, it's time to sit down with the salesperson and negotiate. The critical element of negotiating is recognizing that both the buyer and seller have alternatives. The seller doesn't have to sell to you. But if the salesperson sells the car to you, he cannot sell it to someone else. The opportunity cost of selling the car to you is the foregone profit he would earn by selling the car to someone else. This represents the lowest price he will accept in a deal. As a prospective buyer, you can go elsewhere. If you buy from this dealer, you will not buy the car from another dealer. Thus, your opportunity cost of buying from this dealer is the price you could likely obtain from a competing dealer. This represents the maximum price you would ever pay to this dealer.

Assume you've staked out the inventories at competing dealerships, you've determined your willingness to trade away options for a lower price, and you've researched dealer cost and average regional sales prices through the Internet. You have a good idea of the opportunity cost of buying from this dealer. This represents the maximum you would be willing to pay this dealer for the car. The dealer's costs and the price he expects to get from other prospective buyers represent his opportunity cost of selling to you, and it serves as his minimum price. The price that drives the deal necessarily lies between the opportunity costs of the buyer and seller and will be mutually beneficial.

Let's review that last point again, as it will prove to be the crucial point in understanding the marketplace. *All transactions between a buyer and a seller are mutually beneficial.* If either party believed it would be worse off by making the transaction, no transaction would take place. Thus, to make a profit, your firm must make an offer that's at least as attractive to the consumer as the available alternatives. In essence, then, the only way to maximize profits is to *attract* the consumers' money; to offer a product and price that's at least as desirable as those he would forego if he buys from your firm.

What Does Economics have to Offer to the Business Manager?

Economics studies how individuals deal with scarcity. The theory of the firm is based on the notion that firms seek to maximize profits, but must deal with constraints that inhibit their profitability. The constraints incorporate the opportunity costs of those with whom you wish to do business. The most obvious constraint that confronts a firm is the cost of production. Without production, the firm has nothing to sell, and production costs money. Your firm is going to need workers to produce your good. They expect to be compensated for their time and effort. Clearly, higher salaries for your employees mean less profit for the firm. How much, at a minimum, must you pay them? The wage needed to attract labor is driven by opportunity cost. If an individual works for you, he cannot work for someone else. Hence, if you want to hire a worker, you must offer a salary that's at least as good as what he can get from another employer. The salary does not necessarily have to be identical to what competing employers offer. If your workplace is especially unpleasant or dangerous, you may have to pay a premium to lure the individual to your firm. At the opposite extreme, if your work environment is unusually pleasant or offers desirable perks, you may not have to match competing salaries to attract a workforce. The salient point is that, whatever salary you offer, it's going to be driven by the opportunity cost of the employees you seek to hire.

The same is true for the suppliers of your raw materials. Any item they sell to you cannot be sold to someone else. If you want their business, you must offer a price that's at least as attractive as what they can get from another firm. Note that when it comes to hiring workers or buying materials from prospective suppliers, the opportunity cost of doing business with you drives the wages and prices you must pay.

Beyond the costs of production, the firm's actions are constrained by the opportunity cost of the consumers. From their perspective, the price implies foregone goods and services from other firms. Thus, when consumers see your price, their first instinct is to determine whether they can lower the opportunity costs by buying the identical product at a lower price elsewhere. As a result, the more substitutable your good is, the less flexibility you have in setting a price.

Suppose your good has no identical substitutes. You may have the only BMW dealership within 100 miles of town. Does that give you market power to set a price of your own choosing? Not really. The consumers don't have to buy a BMW; they can buy another make of car. As the only BMW dealer in town, you'll have more flexibility in setting a price than if there were several BMW dealers in the region, but as long as consumers can find *close* substitutes, the opportunity cost of purchasing from you will still influence the price you can charge.

But what if you have no competitors of any kind? To begin with, it's difficult to imagine many circumstances in which **no** substitutes exist. If you owned every car dealer in town, the consumers may deal with out-of-town dealers. If you owned every dealership in the world, consumers might consider buying a bicycle. The price-setting power for the firm increases as the ability to substitute becomes more distant. But the opportunity cost of the consumer still affects the price even if no viable substitute exists. Even without substitutes, the customer doesn't **have** to buy your product. He can choose simply to do without. Thus, even when no apparent substitutes exist, the opportunity cost of the buyer creates boundaries for the price.

It should be obvious that there are innumerable obstacles that can get in the way of profitability, and economists dedicate themselves to studying how profit-seeking firms deal with these constraints. And that's what economics has to offer the business manager. Managers have to the deal with the threat of competition, legal constraints, changing consumer tastes, a complex, evolving labor force, and a myriad of other obstacles. The essence of economics is to determine how to deal with the forces of nature that get in the way of the firm's goals.

But what does economics, or more specifically, managerial economics, have to offer that cannot be found in other business disciplines? Managerial economics should not be viewed as a substitute for other business disciplines. Rather, it serves as the theoretical foundation for the other disciplines. Whereas other business disciplines may tell a manager what to do, the managerial economist will rely on his background as a social scientist to tell you why. A top-selling marketing textbook may list and describe several pricing strategies. A managerial economics textbook will explain when they will work and when they will not. A finance textbook will teach you how to discount future after-tax cash flows to their present value to make capital budgeting decisions. A managerial economics textbook will explain the market forces that will help the manager project the after-tax cash flows as well as the interest rate that should be used to discount the projected income stream.

How Does this Text Differ from Managerial Economics Textbooks?

Now there's a good question! Before I pursued a PhD in economics, I had an MBA and several years of experience with a Fortune 500 company. When I completed the doctorate and began my academic career, I spent many years teaching managerial economics to my MBA classes and became quite familiar with the array of textbooks. Along the way, a family member enrolled in an MBA program and I had a chance to re-familiarize myself with the standard MBA coursework. I began to realize how useful the other courses were, but how useless the managerial economics textbooks were. Not that economics didn't have anything to offer the business manager, rather, most managerial economics textbooks sidestepped issues that business managers would deem useful, and devoted significant space to topics that were far too abstract or esoteric for the manager to use. Indeed, in a survey of over 100 business programs accredited by the Association to Advance Collegiate Schools of Business (AACSB), 54% of the respondents described the economics courses required in their programs as either "unpopular" or "very unpopular." The most common reasons for their lack of popularity were that the economics courses were "too theoretical" (30%), "too difficult" (23%), and "too quantitative" (21%).[1]

None of this surprised me. Most managerial economics textbooks devote an inordinate amount of space to elements of the theory of the firm which, although useful to economics as a social science, are of minimal use to the practicing business manager. Virtually all managerial economics texts, for example, demonstrate that if a firm wishes to maximize production subject to a budget, it will allocate its resources such that the marginal rate of technical substitution is equal to the ratio of input prices. Confused? Would it help if I drew a graph and showed that production would be maximized where the isoquant is tangent to the ratio of the price of labor relative to the price of capital? I didn't think so. I've yet to hear someone from the business community say to me "Boy, I've been sitting on these isoquants all these years, and I never knew what to do with them until I took a course in managerial economics."

The criticism that managerial economics is too quantitative also rings true. There's nothing wrong with quantitative tools. Indeed, MBA programs teach a great number of tools that can help the business manager make better decisions. I teach statistical tools in my managerial economics class that I think will be very helpful to the manager. But what's the point in teaching quantitative skills that business managers will never use? Most managerial economics texts place special emphasis on using algebra and differential calculus to make pricing and output decisions. Curiously, textbooks in the other business disciplines fail to include the use of algebraic equations and calculus to make decisions; in fact, many specifically advise against attempting to do so. To that end, it seems rather illogical to devote time and space to quantitative skills that do not translate particularly well to the real world of the business manager.[2]

The purpose of my contributions to the economics series for Business Expert Press is simple: to bring microeconomic theory into the world of the business manager rather than the other way around. If an element of theory has no practical application, there is no reason to discuss it. Further, if an economic concept does have practical value, it is incumbent upon me to repackage it to suit the manager. In short, my intent is to expound on microeconomic theory that can be taken back to the office and put into use.

Is it necessary for a manager to have a background in economics to read this text? The answer is "no." My objective is to help managers make better decisions, not to preach to economics majors. I assume that many readers may have had a course or two in microeconomics, and some of the more basic concepts may already be familiar to them. But I've written the textbook under the assumption that some readers may never have had an economics course before. For them, it will be necessary for me to start from scratch. Of course, there may be more than a few readers who have had an economics course in their distant past (like during the Dark Ages) who have long forgotten what they'd been taught, and may welcome a quick primer on the more basic concepts.

CHAPTER 2

Consumer Behavior: The Law of Demand and its Effect on Pricing

The Law of Demand

This intent of this textbook is to introduce the manager to innovative pricing strategies that can increase a firm's profit. We will begin by reviewing the basic economic concepts that lead to a single profit-maximizing price. This is based on the assumption that a firm produces a single good and is trying to determine the best price to charge. In setting a price, the firm must consider the *law of demand*. To derive the law of demand, assume that Moe is going to the local high school football game on a Friday night. He has $3.75 in his pocket. For simplicity sake, assume that hot dogs and Cokes are priced at $1.25 each. Moe goes to the concession stand in the middle of the first quarter and must decide whether to buy a hot dog or a Coke. Assume he buys the hot dog. Note that because the price of a hot dog is the same as the price of a Coke, we can infer that Moe gets more satisfaction from the hot dog than he would have obtained from the Coke. Suppose he returns to the concession stand during the second quarter. This time, he must decide between his second hot dog and his first Coke. Let's suppose he buys a second hot dog. Again, by purchasing the second hot dog, he is indicating that he gets more satisfaction from the second hot dog than he does from the first Coke. In the middle of the third quarter, he returns to the concession stand with his last $1.25. Let's assume that this time, he buys a Coke. Again, his buying behavior reveals his preferences; that he obtains more satisfaction from the first Coke than he would have received from the third hot dog.

Economists refer to the additional satisfaction Moe derives from each additional unit of a good as ***marginal utility***. Given that Moe's purchases reveal his preferences, we can conclude the following:

1. Moe prefers the first hot dog to the first Coke
2. Moe prefers the second hot dog to the first Coke
3. Moe prefers the first Coke to the third hot dog

Let's examine the last two revealed preferences: Moe prefers the second hot dog to the first Coke, but he prefers the first Coke to the third hot dog. If both statements are true, the fourth statement logically follows:

4. Moe prefers the second hot dog to the third hot dog

Note that we don't have to ask Moe if he prefers the second hot dog to the third hot dog. Rather, these preferences were revealed through his purchase decisions. The notion that Moe receives less satisfaction from the third hot dog than he does from the second is called ***the law of diminishing marginal utility***. In general, economists assert that as more of a good is consumed, individuals get less satisfaction from each successive unit. If the law of diminishing marginal utility did not exist and Moe had brought $10 to spend on concessions, he would have spent all of his money on hot dogs. The fact that most people do not spend all of their money on one good is implicit proof that the law exists with all of us.

What does the law of diminishing marginal utility mean for firms? Clearly, if each additional hot dog brings less satisfaction to Moe, he would be willing to spend less for each additional hot dog. Suppose Moe would have been willing to spend as much as $2 for the first hot dog, $1.25 for the second hot dog, and $.50 for the third hot dog. Thus, if hot dogs were priced at $.50, Moe would buy three. If the price increased to $1.25, he would only be willing to buy two, and if the price rose to $2, Moe would only buy one. This illustrates the law of demand: the higher the price, the lower the quantity of hot dogs demanded.

Figure 2.1 illustrates Moe's ***demand curve***. The demand curve shows the quantities Moe is willing and able to buy at each price.

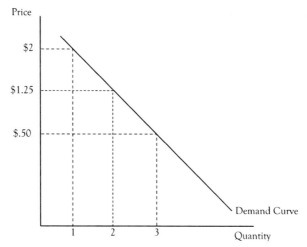

Figure 2.1. Demand curve.

The implications of the law of demand for the firm are inherently obvious. The higher the price of hot dogs, the fewer hot dogs Moe is going to buy. Conversely, the more hot dogs the concession stand wishes to sell, the lower the price it will have to charge.

In July 2011, Netflix created uproar over its announcement to split its DVD-by-mail services and online streaming. Netflix revolutionized the DVD rental business by mailing DVDs to consumers rather than having them browse a local retail outlet. As quality online video streaming developed, the demand for conventional DVD rentals took a steady nosedive. Indeed, Netflix found its own demand for online video streaming to be on the rise, increasing from roughly six million subscribers in 2007 to 25 million in 2011.[1]

But in 2011, Netflix made a strategic decision that incurred the wrath of many subscribers. It decided to separate the two subscription plans entirely. Consumers could subscribe to either the online service or the DVD-by-mail service. To facilitate the move, Netflix renamed its traditional by mail service, Qwikster. Unfortunately, Netflix was more forward-thinking than its customers. Its goal was to split the market segments into separate services and offer a lower price for those who chose to download films. From that perspective, the price of online subscriptions would remain unchanged while the price of DVD-by-mail subscriptions would fall by $2/month.

The subscribers in the dual plan did not see things that way. For $9.99/month, they were able to either rent or download DVDs. To continue with that flexibility, they would have to buy two subscriptions, for a total price of $15.98/month, a whopping 60% increase. With nearly half of its 24.6 million subscribers in the dual plan, the reaction from consumers was one of outrage. Within three months, in response to a marked decline in the number of subscribers, Qwikster was discontinued.

Factors that Cause Demand to Change

A demand curve, such as that illustrated in Figure 2.1, indicates the quantity demanded at any given price. However, the price of that particular good is not the only factor that determines the quantity demanded. We know, for example, that consumer tastes change. If Moe attends the football game on a particularly hot day, he may want more to drink. Given that he only brought $3.75 to the game, he may choose to buy two Cokes and one hot dog rather than two hot dogs and one Coke. We can illustrate the results of his changing tastes graphically. As shown in Figure 2.2, the demand for hot dogs shifts to the left. Whereas Moe had been willing to buy two hot dogs at a price of $1.25, he is now only willing to buy one.

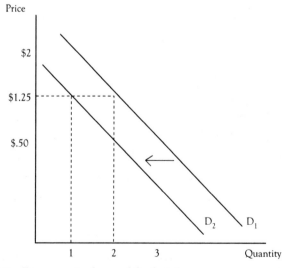

Figure 2.2. Decrease in demand for hot dogs.

The impact of changing tastes on consumer demand explains why department stores frequently have sales on seasonal clothing. As temperatures fall at the end of the summer, the demand for summer clothing decreases. Thus, the quantity of summer clothing demanded at any given price decreases, forcing the firm to lower its price.

This also explains why firms advertise. Advertising can increase the demand for their goods. At any given price, more units can be sold. A classic example of the power of advertising lies in brand name pharmaceuticals. Many pharmaceutical firms obtain patents on drugs when they are first introduced. This gives them the exclusive right to produce and sell the drug for 20 years. Once the patent expires, other pharmaceutical companies can produce identical drugs. To retain its price position, the firm that holds the patent on the drug creates a brand name and spends millions of dollars on advertising to partially insulate its position once the bioequivalent generic brand hits the market. The strategy seems to work: according to the U.S. Food and Drug Administration, despite marketing identical products, brand name drugs are priced 80–85% higher than their generic equivalent.[2]

Changes in the prices of substitute goods can also cause demand to shift. As shown in Figure 2.3, as the price of DVD players decreased in the 1990s, the demand for VCRs decreased.

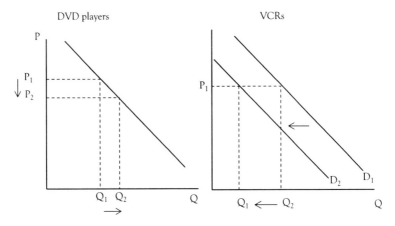

Figure 2.3. Effect of change in the price of a substitute good.

Similarly, when a competitor lowers its price, the demand for your product will decrease. Sometimes a firm manufactures two brands of the same product. Proctor & Gamble manufactures both Cascade and Dawn. Sony produces both laptops and tablets. When the same firm produces substitute goods, a change in the price of one good will affect the demand for the substitute.

If two goods are complementary, a change in the price of one good will affect the demand for the other. A decrease in the price of a laser printer, for example, will increase the demand for ink cartridges, as illustrated in Figure 2.4.

Later in the text, we will explain the significance of complementarity on pricing. For now, let's simply note the fact that in many instances, the price of a laser printer may be the same as the price of two or three ink cartridges refills. Likewise, whereas the price of a razor may be relatively low, the price of the razor-specific blades seems to be quite high. By lowering the price of one good, the demand for the complementary good increases. In the case of the laser printers or razors, the firm holds the price of one good down with the expectation that it will make up for the lost profit margin via the increased demand for the complementary product.

Changes in consumer incomes can also affect demand. An increase in incomes might boost the demand for NBA basketball tickets. Rising

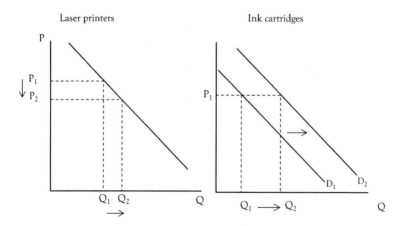

Figure 2.4. Effect of change in price of a complementary good.

incomes do not always cause demand to increase. Increasing incomes may cause the demand for used cars to decrease because consumers would rather buy a new car and can now afford to do so. Economists refer to any good for which demand increases when incomes increase as a *normal good*. When the demand for a good is inversely related to consumer incomes, it is called an *inferior good*.

One should not be misled by the "inferior" tag. Inferior goods are not necessarily low quality products. Few persons would consider a Porsche 970 to be a low-quality car. But if a professional baseball player who currently drives a Porsche signs a five-year $100 million contract and chooses to buy a $387,000 Lamborghini as his next car instead of a Porsche, we can conclude that, for him, the Porsche is an inferior good.

Finally, demand can increase or decrease in response to changes in price expectations. Readers may recall the long gas lines that occurred in the hours following the 9/11 terrorist attacks. Drivers anticipated that the attacks would cause a dramatic spike in fuel prices and showed up en masse to fill up their tanks.

The Law of Demand and Consumer Surplus

A critical concept that arises from the law of demand is called *consumer surplus*. Consumer surplus refers to the difference between the price the consumer is willing to pay and the price he actually pays. Consumers enter the marketplace looking for bargains, which occurs when a consumer buys a good at a lower price than he is willing to pay. Thus, consumer surplus measures the dollar volume of bargains accruing to the consumer.

We can return to Moe's demand curve to measure his consumer surplus. In our original example, each hot dog was priced at $1.25. Because Moe was willing to pay up to $2 for the first hot dog, his consumer surplus for the hot dog is $.75. Similarly, because he was willing to pay up to $1.25 for the second hot dog, he buys the hot dog, but does not gain any additional consumer surplus. Collectively, the value Moe placed on two hot dogs summed to $3.25, but he only spent $2.50, allowing him to retain $.75 in consumer surplus, as shown in Table 2.1.

Table 2.1. Calculating Consumer Surplus

Hot dogs	Willingness to pay $	Price $	Consumer surplus $
1st	2	1.25	2 – 1.25 = .75
2nd	1.25	1.25	1.25 – 1.25 = 0
Total Consumer Surplus: .75			

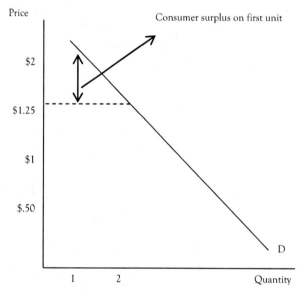

Figure 2.5. Graphical representation of consumer surplus.

Consumer surplus can be represented graphically. For each unit of output, the corresponding point on the demand curve shows the price the individual would be willing to pay for that unit. The vertical distance between the point on the demand curve and the actual price is the consumer surplus for that unit, as shown in Figure 2.5.

We can expand our individual demand curve to derive a market demand curve. Suppose two other consumers (Larry and Curly, of course) also brought money to the football game. Their willingness to pay for hot dogs is summarized in Table 2.2.

Table 2.2. Individual Demands

Hot Dog	Willingness to pay $		
	Moe	Larry	Curly
1st	2	1.75	1.50
2nd	1	0.75	1.25
3rd	0.50	0.25	0.40

Collectively, the consumers' willingness to pay can be used to derive a market demand curve. For example, if the price of a hot dog was $2, Moe would be willing to purchase one hot dog and Larry and Curly would not be willing to buy any. If the price was $1.75, Moe and Larry would each buy one hot dog, but Curly would not purchase any. Hence, at a price of $2, the quantity demanded is one and at $1.75, the quantity demanded is two. Table 2.3 summarizes the market demand curve, which is depicted graphically in Figure 2.6.

Table 2.3. Market Demand

Price $	Quantity demanded
2	1
1.75	2
1.50	3
1.25	4
1	5
0.75	6
0.50	7

We can use the market demand information to determine the concession stand's revenue and the level of consumer surplus. If the concession stand charges $1 for a hot dog, five hot dogs will be purchased. The concession stand will collect $5 in total revenue and consumer surplus will be equal to ($2 − $1) + ($1.75 − $1) + ($1.50 − $1) + ($1.25 − $1) + ($1 − $1), or $2.50.

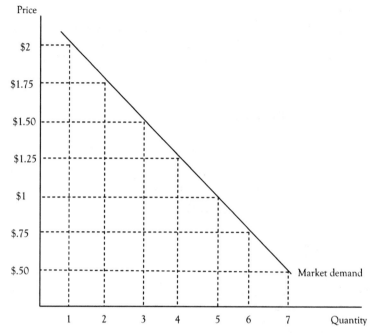

Figure 2.6. Graphical representation of market demand.

Let's take the concession stand example to create a generic graph to illustrate market demand. Because the firm's revenue is equal to price times the quantity demanded, revenue is represented on the graph by the vertical distance between the origin and the price, and the horizontal distance between the origin and the quantity demanded. Consumer surplus, which represents the consumer value that is not captured by the firm, is the area that lies underneath the demand curve, but above the price. This is illustrated in Figure 2.7.

Figure 2.7 succinctly illustrates the world of the single-price firm. At a given price, consumers are willing and able to purchase a given quantity. However, because some consumers would have been willing to pay a higher price for the good, a percentage of the overall value that consumers place on the good goes uncaptured by the firm. In the previous example, one-third of the overall value that Moe, Larry, and Curly placed on hot dogs was not captured. As the chapters develop, we will investigate innovative pricing strategies that attempt to capture consumer surplus.

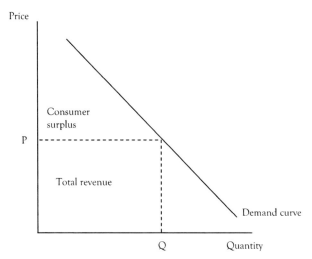

*Figure 2.7. Graphical representation of consumer surplus
and total revenue.*

Summary

- The law of demand is driven by the law of diminishing marginal utility, which states that consumers get less additional satisfaction from each additional unit consumed.
- Because each unit yields less additional satisfaction, the less the consumer is willing to pay consume it.
- The law of demand suggests that, all else equal, the more units the firm wishes to sell, the lower the price it must charge.
- The quantity that a consumer is willing to buy at each price is affected by changes in tastes and preferences, income changes, changes in the prices of substitute and complementary goods, and changes in price expectations.
- Consumer surplus is the difference between the price the consumer is willing to pay and the actual price paid by the consumer. It represents revenue that the firm did not capture that the consumer was, in fact, willing to pay.

CHAPTER 3

Understanding the Price Sensitivity of Buyers

The law of demand asserts that as the price of a good rises, the quantity demanded decreases and vice versa. Another key element of demand theory that is critical to price-setting is the ***price elasticity of demand***. The price elasticity of demand refers to the responsiveness of the quantity demanded to price changes. Drivers inevitably grumble about rising gasoline prices, and for good reason. Many individuals regard driving as a necessity because they simply live too far from work, school, or other valued destinations to walk or ride a bike. Moreover, their cars only run on gas: they can't pump lemonade into their tanks if the price of gas becomes too costly. But consumers are less likely to complain about the rising price of frozen yogurt, and for two reasons. First, frozen yogurt is unlikely to be viewed as a necessity. If the consumer thinks the price is too high, she can simply do without. Moreover, ice cream and frozen custard are reasonably close substitutes for frozen yogurt. Therefore, if the price of frozen yogurt rises, the consumer can purchase the substitute.

Let's illustrate the concept of price elasticity graphically. Figure 3.1 shows the demand curves for gasoline and frozen yogurt. Note that whereas the law of demand holds in both cases, a given increase in the price leads to a larger decrease in the quantity of frozen yogurt demanded relative to the decline in the quantity of gasoline demanded. When the quantity demanded of a given product is relatively responsive to price changes (i.e. frozen yogurt), we say that good has a relatively ***elastic*** demand. When the quantity demanded of a good is not very responsive to price changes (i.e., gasoline), we say the good has a relatively ***inelastic*** demand.

What determines price elasticity? We have already covered two determinants. The first determinant is whether the good is a luxury or a necessity.

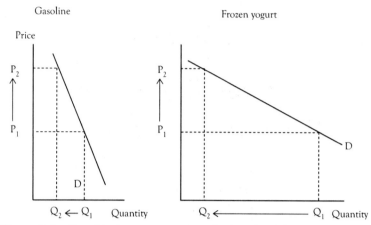

Figure 3.1. *Graphical representation of price elasticity.*

Clearly, if a good is considered to be a luxury, the prospective buyer may choose not to buy it if the price is too high. This is why the travel industry often suffers during recessions. Families are less likely to go on a vacation if one or more of the parents is unemployed or fears losing his job. If the product is viewed as a necessity, on the other hand, the consumer may have no choice but to continue to buy the good.

Another determinant is the availability of substitutes. Consumers look to minimize the opportunity cost of making a purchase. When the price of a good rises, they look for cheaper substitutes. Thus, when the price of frozen yogurt rises, they can substitute into ice cream, whereas the drivers cannot opt for cheaper substitutes when the price of gasoline rises.

This is why gasoline is a frequent government target for taxation. In 1980, the federal gasoline tax was 4 cents per gallon. By 1993, the tax had risen to its current level of 18.4 cents per gallon. And this is only the federal tax. Each state has its own tax, ranging from roughly 10 to 40 cents per gallon.[1] Gasoline is a target for taxation because as a necessity with no viable substitutes, consumers cannot cut back significantly on their gasoline consumption when prices rise.

Another determinant of price elasticity that relates to the availability of substitutes is the definition of the market. For example, whereas consumers may view the demand for gasoline to be relatively inelastic, the same cannot be said for the gasoline sold at the gas station on the corner of First and Main. Clearly, whereas consumers have few alternatives when the price of gasoline rises, they can easily substitute away from the gasoline sold at a specific station by purchasing gas from a competing station. Thus, whereas the demand for gasoline may be inelastic, the demand for gas sold by a specific retailer is highly elastic.

Another determinant of price elasticity is the price of the good as a percentage of the consumer's budget. The National Association for Convenience Stores reported an average gross margin of nearly 47% on warehouse-delivered snack foods at convenience stores in 2008.[2] This should not come as a surprise to consumers. A candy bar that might cost $0.50 at a supermarket may cost $0.75 (50% more) at a convenience store. Why? Undoubtedly, consumers do not make the trip to the convenience store to buy snack foods. In most cases, they enter the store to finalize a gasoline purchase. In deciding whether to buy the candy bar, the consumer is well aware that a better price can be had at a supermarket. But even if the candy bar is cheaper at the supermarket, the opportunity cost of buying it at the convenience store is fairly low, particularly when one considers the time involved in finding a better price. Therefore, we would expect consumers to be relatively price inelastic when it comes to goods that are relatively inexpensive.

Although consumers may claim that they're willing to pay the additional 50% for "convenience," the rationale doesn't really hold up to scrutiny. Suppose a "convenient" auto dealer was selling a new car for $30,000 whereas a competing dealer on the other side of town was offering the identical car for $20,000. Would the consumer be willing to pay the additional 50% for the convenience? Clearly, the difference between paying 50% more for a candy bar as compared to 50% more for a new car is the opportunity cost of the purchase. Regardless of whether the consumer buys the car at the convenient dealership or the one across town, the opportunity cost of the purchase is sizable. Consequently, the higher the price as a percentage of the consumer's budget, the more price sensitive the consumer.

The final determinant of price elasticity is the time the consumer has to make a purchase. Consider an extreme case. The National Weather

Service reports that a hurricane is imminent. When that occurs, coastal residents are in a rush to buy plywood hurricane shutters, install them quickly, and drive inland before the storm makes landfall. Under less trying circumstances, these same consumers would shop around for an acceptable price. With the hurricane due to arrive in a matter of hours, consumers have minimal opportunity to compare prices and may feel compelled to make a hasty purchase. Clearly, this gives a great deal more market power to the supplier of plywood, whose price need not be as competitive as it might have been during less urgent periods.

The importance of time as a determinant of price sensitivity should not be underestimated by firms. Because the price of a good represents opportunity cost, buyers constantly seek ways to minimize the opportunity cost of a purchase. Firms that foolishly believe they have the advantage over consumers will eventually find that buyers found a way to lower their opportunity costs. When the price of gas increased by $0.86/gallon between the spring of 2010 and 2011, both Toyota and Honda reported significant increases in Prius and Insight sales.[3] Clearly, most consumers are not in a position to buy a new car when gas prices rise. However, if fuel prices remain high, over time, consumers will look seriously at hybrids when they need a new vehicle. In summary, then, the longer the time the consumer has to make a purchase decision, the more elastic the demand for the good.

How can knowledge of price elasticity help a firm make better pricing decisions? To begin with, we need to find a way to measure price elasticity. Because the law of demand holds regardless of whether the good has an elastic or inelastic demand, how do we distinguish one from the other? Because price elasticity refers to the responsiveness of the quantity demanded to price changes, the degree of responsiveness can be measured. Economists measure price elasticity as

$$E_p = \% \text{ change in quantity purchased}/\% \text{ change in price}$$

In measuring price elasticity, note that "quantity purchased" is used instead of "quantity demanded." Although the intent is to equate the two, this may not always be the case. If the firm stocks out of an item, the quantity demanded may exceed the quantity purchased. For firms trying to measure price elasticity, this is an important consideration. If the quantity demanded exceeds the quantity purchased due to stockouts, the results may delude managers into thinking consumers are less price sensitive than they actually are.

Because the law of demand suggests that the quantity demanded decreases as prices rise, E_p is negative. The convention among many economists is to ignore the negative sign. In terms of measuring price elasticity, economists define "elastic" as any situation in which the percentage change in the quantity demanded exceeds the percentage change in the price. Based on the equation, then, if the good has a relatively elastic demand, the elasticity coefficient will be greater than one. For example, an elasticity coefficient of 2.5 means that each 1% change in the price leads to a 2.5% change in the quantity demanded. "Inelastic demand" is just the reverse: economists say that a good has a relatively inelastic demand if the percentage change in the quantity demanded is less than the percentage change in the price. In such cases, the elasticity coefficient will be less than one. For instance, if the elasticity coefficient is equal to 0.4, a 1% change in the price leads to a 0.4% change in the quantity demanded. If the percentage change in the quantity demanded is equal to the percentage change in the price (i.e. a 10% price increase leads to a 10% decrease in the quantity demanded), the good is exhibiting *unitary* elasticity. The definitions are summarized in Table 3.1.

The coefficient is more precisely measured as

$$EP = \frac{(\text{New quantity} - \text{old quantity}) / (\text{Average of the two quantities})}{(\text{New price} - \text{old price}) / (\text{Average of the two prices})}$$

Note that the respective denominators in calculating percentage changes are the average of the two quantities (or prices) rather than the original quantity (or price). This is to assure that the coefficient

Table 3.1. Measuring and Defining Elasticity

(1)	If $E_p > 1$, demand is elastic (i.e. relatively responsive to price changes)
(2)	If $E_p < 1$, demand is inelastic (i.e. relatively unresponsive to price changes)
(3)	If $E_p = 1$, demand is unitary (i.e. percentage change in price equals percentage change in quantity)

corresponding to a given price change along a demand curve will be the same regardless of whether the price increases or decreases. For example, suppose a firm increases the price from 5 to $11, and as a result, the quantity demanded decreases from six to two units. If the percentage change in the price was measured as the change in the price divided by the original price, the percentage change would be equal to 120%. If, on the other hand, the price decreased from 11 to $5, the percentage change in the price would be equal to 54.5%. By dividing the price change by the average of the two prices, the percentage change will be the same regardless of whether the original price was $5 or $11. This assures that the calculated price elasticity coefficient will be the same regardless of whether the price increases or decreases.

When calculating the price elasticity of demand, firms should be cognizant of the fact that the two price/quantity combinations may not lie on the same demand curve. Figure 3.2 illustrates the problem that may arise. The graph on the left shows two price/quantity combinations. When using the numbers to calculate the price elasticity of demand, the firm assumes they lie on the same demand curve. The graph on the right shows another possibility. One of the other determinants of demand (i.e. the price of substitutes) may have changed, causing the demand curve to shift. If the price/quantity combinations lie on different demand curves, the elasticity coefficient will be biased and could provide misleading pricing implications. One should note that the scenario on the right is quite likely to be the case. Managers usually do not change prices randomly.

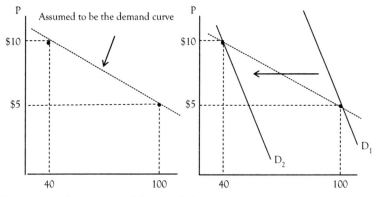

Figure 3.2. Incorrect inference of elasticity.

More often than not, the price change was motivated by a change in a factor that can shift a demand curve, such as the price charged by competing firms. Later in this text, when we discuss dynamic pricing and e-commerce, we will see opportunities for firms to obtain more accurate measures of price elasticity.[4]

The relationship between price elasticity and revenue is important. For example, suppose a firm raises its price from 5 to $10 and the quantity demanded falls from 100 to 60 units. In this case, raising the price caused the firm's revenue to increase from 500 to $600. Suppose, however, that in response to the price increase, the quantity demanded falls from 100 to 40 units. In this circumstance, the price increase caused revenues to fall from 500 to $400. Figure 3.3 illustrates the distinction. Note that the demand curve that corresponds to the decrease in revenues is more elastic than the demand curve that is associated with an increase in revenues.

When we reflect on the definitions of elastic and inelastic in Table 3.1, the relationship between elasticity and revenue should become fairly obvious. We define demand as "elastic" if the percentage change in quantity exceeds the percentage change in price. Hence, for example, if the price

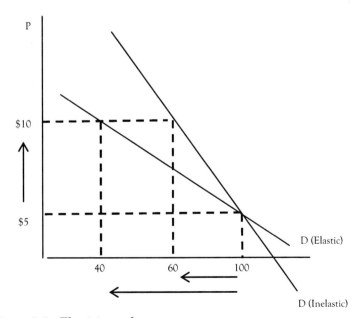

Figure 3.3. Elasticity and revenue.

rises by 10%, the quantity demanded will fall by more than 10%, which implies that revenue will decrease. If, on the other hand, the price declines by 10%, the quantity demanded will rise by more than 10%. This suggests that revenues will increase in response to the price cut. In general, therefore, when the demand is elastic, price and revenue will move in opposite directions.

If demand is relatively inelastic, the percentage change in the quantity demanded will be less than the percentage change in the price. Thus, if the price rises by 10%, the quantity demanded will fall by less than 10%, causing revenue to rise. If the price falls by 10%, the quantity demanded will rise by less than 10%, leading to a decrease in revenue. If demand is inelastic, therefore, price and revenue will move in the same direction.

Finally, if demand is unitary, a given percentage change in the price will lead to an identical percentage change in the quantity demanded. For example, a 10% price hike will lead to a 10% decline in the quantity demanded. The two percentage changes cancel out, causing revenues to remain the same. Table 3.2 summarizes the relationship between elasticity and revenue.

Although many persons (economists included) tend to label a good as having either an elastic demand for an inelastic demand, the elasticity depends on the price. If we examine the demand schedule in Table 3.3 and calculate the price elasticity of demand between each pair of prices, the results are illuminating.

As Table 3.3 indicates, the price elasticity of demand is not constant across all prices. Between $3 and $5, demand is inelastic. Between $5 and $6, demand is unitary, and demand is elastic for prices above $6. We can also see that as we move up the demand curve, the coefficient becomes increasingly elastic.

Table 3.2. Relationship between Elasticity and Revenue

(1) Elastic:	% change in QD > % change in P	Price and revenue move in opposite directions
(2) Inelastic:	% change in QD < % change in P	Price and revenue move in the same direction
(3) Unitary:	% change in QD = % change in P	Revenue will not change if the price changes

Table 3.3. Price Elasticities Along the
Demand Curve

Price $	Quantity	Elasticity coefficient
8	3	2.14
7	4	1.44
6	5	1
5	6	0.69
4	7	0.47
3	8	

This revelation should not be too surprising. We used snack foods at a convenience store to illustrate why the price of snack foods could be 50% higher than at a supermarket without causing sales to suffer dramatically. Let's assume that the manager of the store increased the price of a candy bar from $0.50 to $0.75. Although the number of candy bars sold decreased after the price hike, revenues increased. This would indicate that the candy bars had an inelastic demand. The manager would be foolish to believe that candy bars would have an inelastic demand at all prices. If consumers were relatively insensitive to candy bar prices, and price increases were inevitably accompanied by rising revenue, then the manager would think that charging $25 for a candy bar would yield far greater revenues than $0.75. Clearly, the store would be hard-pressed to sell *any* candy bars at a price of $25. It stands to reason, then, that somewhere between $0.75 and $25, the demand goes from being inelastic to elastic.

Let's see how the relationship between elasticity and the demand curve affects pricing. Theory suggests that demand tends to be relatively inelastic at lower prices, becomes unitary at a higher price, and eventually becomes elastic at even higher prices. Earlier, we stated that if the current price is in the inelastic portion of a demand curve, an increase in the price will cause revenues to rise. On the other hand, if the current price is the in elastic section of the demand curve, decreasing the price will cause revenues to rise. Taken together, this implies that the firm will maximize revenues by setting its price in the unitary section of the demand curve. This is shown in Figure 3.4. As the price moves toward P*, revenues rise. Total revenues are maximized by setting the price in the unitary section of the demand curve. At that price, Q* units are demanded.

Of course, firms are interested in maximizing profits, not revenues. Although an understanding of price elasticity is critical to the decision-maker, the scenario exhibited in Figure 3.4 will also maximize profits if the firm has no variable costs. This is likely to be the case for setting ticket prices. The seats already exist; the relevant decision is what price to charge. Because variable costs will not change as more tickets are sold, the firm seeks the ticket price that will maximize revenues. In doing so, it will also maximize profits. Note that in this context, the ticket seller may actually be more profitable by leaving seats empty than by lowering the price to assure a sellout. Later, we will discuss pricing strategies that would allow the firm to sell every seat without suffering a decline in profits.

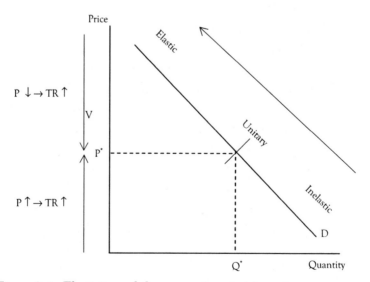

Figure 3.4. Elasticity and the revenue-maximizing price.

Cross Price Elasticity of Demand

Another important elasticity concept is the cross price elasticity of demand. Often, a firm may offer complementary or substitute goods in its product lines. At Burger King, French fries and soft drinks are complements to hamburgers. Proctor & Gamble's (P&G) line of laundry detergents include Tide, Cheer, and Bold. Although they are all P&G brands, consumers view them as substitutes. When a firm has product lines that serve as either complements or substitutes for other lines, a change in the price of one good might affect the unit sales of the other good. An increase in the price of hamburgers at Burger King may decrease not only the quantity of hamburgers demanded, but also the quantity of fries demanded. This is illustrated in Figure 3.5.

The cross price elasticity of demand is a means to measure the sensitivity of unit sales of one good to changes in the price of a related good. It is calculated as

E_C = % change in the quantity of good Y purchased/% change in the price of good X,

where goods X and Y are either substitutes or complements. In evaluating the coefficient, the primary difference between the cross price elasticity of demand and the standard price elasticity coefficient is that the latter is, by definition negative (price and quantity are inversely related

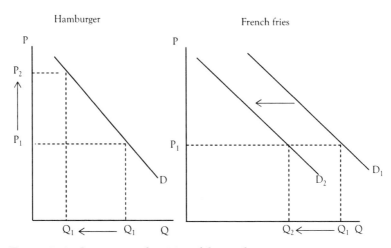

Figure 3.5. Cross price elasticity of demand.

on the demand curve). Therefore, economists usually ignore the negative sign. In contrast, the cross price elasticity of demand can be either positive or negative, depending on the relationship between X and Y. If the two goods are complementary, an increase in the price of X will cause the unit sales of Y to fall, implying a negative cross-elasticity coefficient. For example, if the estimated cross-elasticity coefficient is –3, a 1% increase in the price of X will lead to a 3% decrease in the unit sales of the complementary product. If X and Y are substitutes, an increase in the price of X will result in increased unit sales of Y. In this case, the cross-elasticity coefficient will be positive. As an example, a cross-elasticity coefficient of 0.85 implies that a 1% increase in the price of X will cause the unit sales of the substitute good, Y, to increase by 0.85%.

The cross-elasticity coefficient can be useful to determine the degree of complementarity or substitutability across product lines. Suppose, for example, that the cross-elasticity coefficient that measures the responsiveness of French fry sales to changes in hamburger prices is –4. In contrast, suppose the coefficient that measures the responsiveness of ice cream sundaes to changes in hamburger prices is –0.10. The first scenario implies that each 1% increase in the price of hamburgers decrease the quantity of French fries sold by 4% whereas, in the second case, a 1% increase in the price of hamburgers causes ice cream sundae sales to fall by 0.10%. Together, these coefficients imply that fries are a much closer complement to hamburger sales than are ice cream sundae sales.

The same type of comparisons can be made for product lines that are potentially substitutes for each other. The cross-elasticity coefficient that measures the responsiveness of chicken sandwich sales to changes in hamburger prices may be 1.5, whereas the responsiveness of salad sales to changes in hamburger prices may be 0.3. One would infer from these coefficients that chicken sandwiches are considered by customers to be closer substitutes for hamburgers than salads.

Summary

- The price elasticity of demand refers to the responsiveness of the quantity demanded to price changes. It is measured by the percentage change in the quantity demanded divided by the percentage change in the price.

- The degree to which consumers respond to price changes depends on whether the good is a luxury or a necessity, the degree to which substitutes are available, the broadness of the definition of the market, the price of the good as a percentage of the consumer's income, and the time the consumer has to make the purchase.
- If the percentage change in the quantity demanded exceeds the percentage change in the price, demand is deemed to be relatively elastic. Price changes and revenue changes will move in opposite directions.
- If the percentage change in the quantity demanded is less than the percentage change in the price, demand is deemed to be relatively inelastic. Price changes and revenue changes will move in the same direction.
- If the percentage change in the quantity demanded is the same as the percentage change in the price, demand is deemed to be unitary elastic. Price changes within this range will not affect revenues.
- As the price rises, demand becomes increasingly elastic. It moves from an inelastic section to a unitary section to an elastic section. The firm's revenues will be maximized by setting the price in the unitary section.
- The cross price elasticity of demand measures the responsiveness of the quantity demanded of one good to price changes in a related good, such as a substitute or complementary good. It is measured as the percentage change in the quantity demanded of good X divided by the percentage change in the price of good Y.

CHAPTER 4

One Perfect Price: Profit Maximization for the Single Price Firm

Ultimately, the purpose of this textbook is to develop innovative pricing strategies designed to capture consumer surplus. But prior to devising such strategies, we must first derive the profit-maximizing strategy for the single-price firm so we have a basis for comparison.

Let's assume Wendy has created her own interior design business. To start her business, she purchased interior design software for $1000 that would allow prospective clients to visualize her ideas. She also bought an assortment of wallpaper, carpet, and paint samples for $500. Of course, each individual job will incur additional costs. Although the cost and price of each job would vary in real life, we will assume the costs associated with each job are equal to $550 and she will charge a flat fee to each client.

The costs of the software and samples are considered to be *fixed costs* because they will not vary with the number of jobs Wendy takes on. Moreover, if she has already purchased the software and samples and cannot return them for a partial refund, they constitute *sunk costs*, meaning they cannot be recovered. Wendy's first decision is to determine whether she could take on her first job. If this were to be her one and only job, she could scour the marketplace and find the individual is willing to pay the most for her services. As not all interior designers are alike, Wendy faces competition but retains some flexibility to set her own price.

Suppose Wendy finds a customer who is willing to pay $1300. Should Wendy take on the job? At first glance, one may say "no." After all, she has already expended $1500 on the samples and software, and the job will cost an additional $550. But this is where the significance of sunk costs comes into play. Assuming she cannot return the samples or re-sell the software, if she turns down the job, her business will suffer a $1500 loss. But if she takes the job, she expends an additional $550, collects an additional $1300, and her overall loss falls from $1500 to $750. By agreeing to the job, her losses decrease by $750. Economists argue that because sunk costs cannot be recovered, they should be ignored in decision-making. In Wendy's case, the only factors that are relevant to the decision are the additional costs the job will incur and the additional revenues it will generate. The $550 cost of completing the job is called a **variable cost** because it represents an expenditure that varies with the number of jobs completed. Alternatively, economists label the additional cost of each additional job as its **marginal cost.** Clearly, Wendy should agree to the job if she can get a price that exceeds $550.[1] Therefore, because the client is willing to pay $1300 for the job, Wendy will profit by $750 by agreeing to the work.

The law of demand suggests that the more jobs Wendy wants to take on, the lower the price she will have to charge. Again, for the time being, we will assume that Wendy plans to charge all of her customers the same price. If Wendy wants to perform two jobs, she will have to lower her price for both clients. Suppose she decides she can attract two clients if she charges a price of $1200. Is it worth her while? At face value, the answer is "yes". The second job will cost $550, so if she can get a price of $1200, she adds $650 to her overall profits. But is this really the case? Let's do some simple math: if she only performs one job, her revenues will equal $1300 and her variable costs will total $550, leaving a profit contribution of $750. If she decides to do two jobs, her revenues will be $2400 and her variable costs will sum to $1100. Note that the second job increased her overall profits by only $550, not $750.

Why did her profits rise by only $550? To understand, let's examine the full ramifications of her decision making. If she only agrees to one job, she can charge her client $1300. If she decides to do two jobs (and under the assumption that all of her clients will be charged the same price), she will charge $1200 for **each** job. Although she gains an extra $1200 in revenue from the second job, the revenue she could have earned from the first job falls from $1300 to $1200. In understanding the ramifications from the revenue side, the additional $1200 is referred to as the *output effect*. It represents the revenue she will receive from the second job. The $100 price cut on the first job is referred to as the *price effect*. Economists refer to the additional revenue generated from an additional unit (or job, in this case) as the *marginal revenue*. The marginal revenue from performing two jobs instead of one is equal to the sum of the output and price effects. Put another way, although the second job is priced at $1200, if Wendy decides to do it, her revenues only increase by $1100 ($2400 from two jobs less the $1300 she could have earned from one job). Thus, the marginal revenue from the second job is $1100.

In essence, when considering whether to perform two jobs instead of one, she need only ask two questions: by how much will her costs rise if she performs the job (marginal cost), and by how much will her revenues rise if she performs the extra job (marginal revenue)? In this case, if she decides to do two jobs, the additional (marginal) cost is $550 and the additional (marginal) revenue is $1100. Hence, her profits will rise by $550 if she does the second job. (In this case, because her business is not yet profitable if she only agrees to two jobs, her losses will decline by $550).

Table 4.1 summarizes the potential jobs Wendy can take on. As the table illustrates, each job can be evaluated by comparing its marginal revenue and marginal cost.

As the table indicates, the marginal revenue from each of the first four jobs exceeds the marginal cost. Wendy would not be willing to take on five jobs because the marginal cost ($550) exceeds the marginal revenue ($500).

Table 4.1. Finding the Profit-Maximizing Price and Quantity Using Marginal Revenue and Marginal Cost

Jobs	Price	Total revenue $	Marginal revenue $	Total cost $	Marginal cost $	Total profit $
0	–	0	–	1500	–	(1500)
1	1300	1300	1300	2050	550	(750)
2	1200	2400	1100	2600	550	(200)
3	1100	3300	900	3150	550	150
4	1000	4000	700	3700	550	300
5	900	4500	500	4250	550	250
6	800	4800	300	4800	550	0

We can also use the data in Table 4.1 to calculate the consumer surplus. Wendy is charging her clients the profit-maximizing price of $1000. However, we know that one of her clients was willing to pay $1300, one was willing to pay $1200, and a third was willing to pay $1100. By charging all four clients $1000, Wendy is missing out on $600 in consumer surplus.

Figure 4.1 illustrates the single price strategy. Due to the price effect, the marginal revenue from an additional job is less than the price of the job (except for the initial one). Therefore, the marginal revenue curve lies below the demand curve. Because we assumed the marginal cost of each job to be constant, the marginal cost curve is a horizontal line.

Figure 4.1 shows the marginal revenue for each of the first four jobs exceeds the marginal cost. Beginning with the fifth job, marginal cost is greater than marginal revenue. The demand curve indicates that the four jobs can be sold at a price of $1000. Figure 4.2 focuses on consumer surplus. As the graph indicates, the consumer surplus on the first job is $300, the consumer surplus on the second job is $200, and the consumer surplus on the third job is $100. The client for the fourth job retains no consumer surplus.

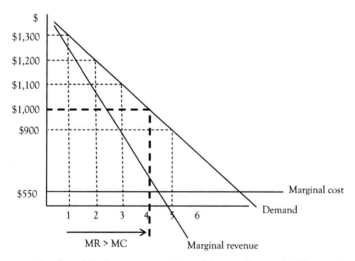

Figure 4.1. Graphical representation of the profit-maximizing price and quantity.

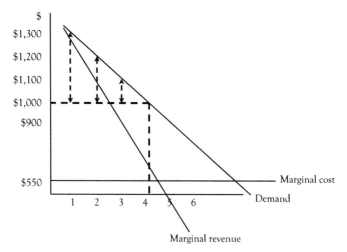

Figure 4.2. The profit-maximizing quantity and consumer surplus.

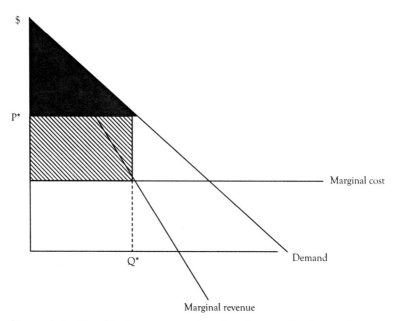

Figure 4.3. Graphical representation of profit contribution and consumer surplus at the profit-maximizing quantity.

Figure 4.3 combines Figures 4.1 and 4.2 into a single generic graph. The firm has an incentive to produce until the point where the marginal revenue is equal to the marginal cost (i.e. it produces every unit for which marginal revenue exceeds marginal cost, but produces no unit whose marginal cost is greater than its marginal revenue. The corresponding profit-maximizing price (P*) is indicated by the demand curve: it shows the highest price that would allow the firm to sell the profit-maximizing quantity (Q*). The shaded area illustrates the consumer surplus and the striped area is the firm's profit contribution.

Summary

- Marginal revenue is the change in revenue associated with a given change in output. Marginal revenue has two components: the output effect, which is the revenue generated by the additional units of output; and the price effect, which is the revenue lost on previous units due to the price reductions necessary to sell more units.
- If the revenue generated by the additional units (i.e. output effect) exceeds the lost revenue on the other units due to the price reduction (i.e. price effect), marginal revenue is greater than zero. Increased production will lead to more revenue.
- If the revenue generated by the additional units (i.e. output effect) is less than the lost revenue on the other units due to the price reduction (i.e. price effect), marginal revenue is less than zero. Increased production will cause total revenues to fall.
- Marginal cost refers to any change in costs that are associated with an increase in production. Marginal costs are, by definition, variable costs.
- If the marginal revenue associated with an increase in production exceeds its marginal costs, the firm's profits will rise (or its losses will become smaller).
- If the marginal cost associated with an increase in production exceeds its marginal revenue, the firm's profits will fall (or its losses will rise).
- Under a single price strategy, uncaptured consumer surplus will exist.

PART II

Different Strokes for Different Folks: Charging More Than One Price for the Same Good

CHAPTER 5

If You Could Read My Mind: First-Degree Price Discrimination Strategies

Readers are probably a step or two ahead of me. Why, one may ask, does Wendy have to charge all four clients the same price? Can't she negotiate prices with each client individually? Indeed, she probably can. If she does, Wendy is engaging in *price discrimination*. Price discrimination is the practice of charging different prices to different customers. Before we elaborate, let's first identify what would not constitute price discrimination. In our simplified example, we assumed the cost of each job was identical. In the context of interior design, this isn't a very realistic assumption. Some clients will want more elaborate design jobs than others. Consequently, one can reasonably expect that the price Wendy charges each client will be based on the cost of the job. This would not constitute price discrimination because the price variations across customers are based on cost differences across customers. Price discrimination exists when the price differences are unrelated to cost differences; that the firm charges different prices to different customers because of differences in their willingness to pay. In essence, price discrimination is based on what we saw in Figure 4.1: that under a single price strategy, some consumers are willing to pay more than the profit-maximizing price. Hence, these customers walk away with consumer surplus that the firm cannot capture with a single price. Price discrimination is an attempt to capture some or the entire consumer surplus.

The most extreme form of price discrimination is **first-degree price discrimination** (sometimes called **perfect price discrimination**). Under first-degree price discrimination, each unit is sold for the highest price the market will bear. We can examine first-degree price discrimination by looking at the numbers in Table 5.1. We already determined that one

Table 5.1. First-Degree Price Discrimination

Jobs	Price $	Total revenue $	Marginal revenue $	Total cost $	Marginal cost $	Total profit $
0	–	0	–	1,500	–	(1,500)
1	1,300	1,300	1,300	2,050	550	(750)
2	1,200	2,500	1,200	2,600	550	(100)
3	1,100	3,600	1,100	3,150	550	450
4	1,000	4,600	1,000	3,700	550	900
5	900	5,500	900	4,250	550	1,250
6	800	6,300	800	4,800	550	1,500

of Wendy's clients would have been willing to pay as much as $1,300 for the job, a second would have been willing to pay $1,200, a third would have been willing to pay as much as $1,100 for the work, and a fourth was willing to pay no more than $1,000. Quite obviously, then, rather than to charge each client $1,000, she should negotiate with each buyer individually and extract the highest price each person is willing to pay. Instead of bringing in $4,000 in revenue, Wendy would collect $4,600, and her profits would rise from $300 to $600.

In fact, using a first-degree price discrimination strategy, Wendy's profits would increase by much more than $600. To illustrate, let's go back to the single-price strategy exhibited earlier. Recall that Wendy opted to charge a price of $1,000 and take on no more than four jobs. Why did she decide against the fifth job? Because, as Table 4.1 indicated, the marginal cost of the fifth job ($550) exceeded the marginal revenue ($500). If she decided to go with the fifth job, her profit contribution would decrease by $50. But is this still the case?

Let's go back to Table 4.1 and re-examine the marginal revenue from the fifth job. Recall that the marginal revenue was composed of the output effect and the price effect. The output effect consisted of the revenue generated by that specific job. In this instance, the job could be performed at a price of $900. The price effect refers to the foregone revenue from the other four jobs owing to the price cut. If Wendy took on four jobs, the price charged to each of the four clients would have been $1,000. By taking on five jobs, the price charged to those clients falls to $900. Therefore, the price effect is –$100 times four jobs, or –$400. By taking on five jobs instead of four, Wendy's revenue increases by $500 (the sum of the output and price effects), which is not sufficient to cover the marginal cost of $550.

But note how this changes with first-degree price discrimination. Because Wendy negotiates with each client individually, she can lower the price to $900 for the fifth client without reducing it for the other four clients. In other words, with first-degree price discrimination, there is no price effect. Put another way, with first-degree price discrimination, the marginal revenue of each job is equal to the price charged for that job. Therefore, Wendy will be willing to take on the job if the price is sufficient to cover the cost of the job.

Let's re-produce Wendy's demand schedule and make the necessary adjustments to show the full ramifications of first-degree price discrimination. Recall that with the single-price strategy, Wendy took on four jobs, charged a price of $1,000, earned a profit of $300, but was unable to capture consumer surplus totaling $600.

With first-degree price discrimination, Wendy will take on every job for which the price is sufficient to cover its cost. As the table indicates, all six jobs carry price tags that exceed the cost of the work. Consequently, Wendy will opt to do all six jobs and increase her profits from 300 to $1,500. In fact, because the table is truncated at six jobs, Wendy could probably increase her profits well beyond $1,500. In effect, she will take on every job that she can price above $550.

Let's compare Tables 4.1 and 5.1 to see why Wendy is willing to take on more jobs with first-degree price discrimination. Under a single-price strategy, she was not willing to perform the fifth job because the marginal revenue ($500) was less than the marginal cost of the job ($550). Note, however, that the fifth job, in and of itself, could have been performed at a profit. The cost of the job is $550 and the client was willing to pay her $900 for the work. The only reason Wendy declined to perform it was due to the price effect; despite the fact that the job could have turned a profit, she wasn't willing to take it on if it was going to require her to drop her price from 1,000 to $900 for the other four clients.

Notice how this changes under first-degree price discrimination. Because there is no price effect, Wendy is not concerned that by dropping her price for the fifth client, she will have to lower her price for the other four. As long as that job can be priced at a profit, the job is worth accepting.

Beyond leading to a greater number of jobs and increased profits, one can see the effect of price discrimination on consumer surplus. Under a single-price strategy, $600 worth of consumer surplus went uncaptured. With first-degree price discrimination, each customer pays the highest price that he is willing to bear; consequently, consumer surplus is equal to zero. No consumer surplus goes uncaptured.

Figure 5.1 illustrates the effects of first-degree price discrimination graphically. Since there is no price effect, the marginal revenue is the same as the price of the good. Therefore, unlike with the single-price strategy, there is no marginal revenue curve that lies below the demand curve. Rather, the marginal revenue curve and the demand curve are one and the same.

Notice that in Figure 5.1, the marginal revenue of all six units exceeds their marginal cost. This is because each of the six units can be sold at a profit. Wendy would be willing to take on all six jobs, and more: Q* represents the profit-maximizing quantity. Note also that because each consumer is charged the highest price he is willing to pay, there is no consumer surplus. Instead, the entire area that lies between the demand curve and the marginal cost curve constitutes her profit contribution, shown as the shaded area in the more generic graph in Figure 5.2.

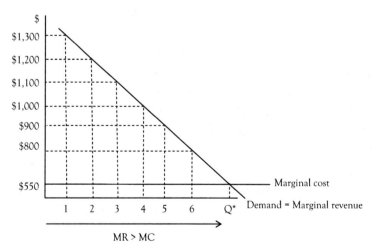

Figure 5.1. Graphical representation of first-degree price discrimination.

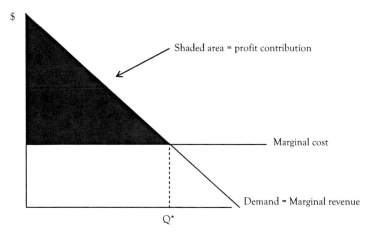

Figure 5.2. First-degree price discrimination and the profit-maximizing output.

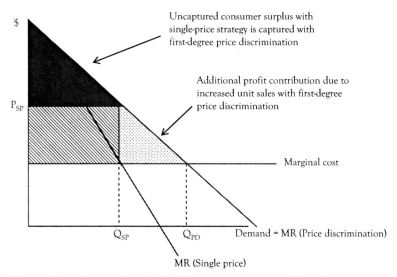

Figure 5.3. Comparing the single-price strategy and first-degree price discrimination.

Figure 5.3 shows a generic graph that contrasts first-degree price discrimination with the single price strategy. As the figure indicates, the profit-maximizing output is greater with first-degree price discrimination (Q_{PD}) than under the single price strategy (Q_{SP}). The dark shaded area represents consumer surplus that is not captured under the single price strategy, but is transferred to the firm with first-degree price discrimination. And whereas the lined area represents the profit contribution using the single price strategy, the profit contribution with first-degree price discrimination is the sum of the shaded, striped, and dotted areas.

Now that we've examined first-degree price discrimination from a theoretical perspective, let's translate it into practical application. Note my choice of examples: an interior designer. I used this example for several reasons. First, Wendy gets to decide how many jobs she wants to perform. In contrast, most manufacturers make production decisions in lot sizes or batches. Few can make production decisions one unit at a time.[1] Second, Wendy is in a position to negotiate the price of each job individually with her clients if she wishes to do so. In a standard production environment, each unit that appears on the shelf of the retailer will carry the same price tag, although prices may vary somewhat across retailers. Third, Wendy is likely to have at least some semblance of market power. The tastes and skills are likely to vary across interior designers. If clients are "brand loyal" to Wendy, she need not have to match the price offered by her competitors. She does, however, have to be cognizant of the prices charged by the competition. If she asks too much, even the most loyal of customers might go elsewhere. The demand curve used in the exercise was based on the assumption that the clients' willingness to pay Wendy factored in the degree of substitutability across designers and the prices charged by the others.

We often see attempts at first-degree price discrimination practiced at car dealerships. Although each car has a sticker price, most buyers are aware than they can bargain with the salesperson for a better price. Because the salesperson receives a commission on the sale of a car, he attempts to gauge each buyer's willingness to pay. The more the buyer gushes over how much he loves the car, the better the price the salesperson is likely to extract. If the prospective buyer demonstrates knowledge of the invoice price, the availability of similar cars in the region, and most importantly, the degree to which he considers vehicles at other dealerships to be an adequate substitute for this model at this particular dealership, the better the price the consumer is likely to get. In any event, a dealer may sell ten identical models to ten different customers at ten different prices.

The University of Alabama athletic department implements a unique form of first-degree price discrimination. A common practice among

college athletic departments is to offer special perks, such as priority seat-
ing or personalized parking, for persons who donate to the department.
Typically, the perks associated with specific donation amounts are pub-
licized in a brochure or web site. But Alabama's Tide Totals program ups
the ante. Donors receive points based on various categories associated
with dollar donations and the longevity of such donations. Each year, the
donors are ranked in points from highest to lowest, with the priorities in
divvying out perks based on points. So how much must one donate to
assure one's self first dibs for a ticket to a major bowl game involving the
Crimson Tide? Answer: more than anyone else. By substituting a point
system for perks tied to fixed dollar donations, the athletic department
pits fan against fan, competing for the top priorities. In doing so, the
department is able to recoup quite a bit of consumer surplus. In fact,
according to its website, the Crimson Tide athletic department attracted
more than $20 million in donations when it first instituted the program
in 2006.[2]

Private colleges also engage in first-degree price discrimination. The
posted tuition and fees are the equivalent of a sticker price on a new
car. The high price is used to signal a higher quality product. Financial
aid budgets to determine "merit-based aid" are, in fact, student-specific
price discounts based on the applicant's inferred willingness to pay. An
estimated 60% of private colleges and universities use statistical formulas
to determine financial aid offers.[3] Some schools "strongly recommend"
a campus visit, use the visits to infer interest and commitment, and
then extend less generous aid offers to those students. Many private colleges offer an "early admission" program. The application is fast-tracked
through the admissions process with the proviso that the student will not
choose another school if admitted. This effectively eliminates price competition and can result in lower financial aid offers. Some schools even
determine aid based on the student's planned major. A student at Johns
Hopkins University learned that he would have received a more generous
aid offer if he had indicated a desire to major in the humanities rather
than premed.[4] In most cases, prospective students can appeal the financial
aid offer, but this is rarely advertised up front. Applicants who claim to
have received better offers elsewhere are usually requested to fax the proof
before the appeal is heard.

The airline industry has turned first-degree price discrimination into a near art form. Until 1978, airfares were regulated by the Civil Aeronautics Board (CAB). The fare for a given route was set by the CAB. After the Airline De-Regulation Act passed in 1978, the airlines were free to set their own prices, and quickly recognized the benefits of first-degree price discrimination. By and large, the costs associated with a given flight are fixed. The cost for fuel and flight staff are the same regardless of how many passengers are on the plane. The variable cost associated with the number of passengers is negligible (i.e. the cost of a soft drink, napkin, small package of pretzels, etc.). Under a single-price strategy, the airline had to determine the one price that would maximize profits. If the plane had 125 seats, it might be worthwhile to sell tickets to 75 customers if lowering the price to fill the plane caused overall profits to fall (i.e. if the price effect resulting from lowering the price on the first 75 seats exceeded the output effect of selling 50 additional tickets). But airline de-regulation eliminated any legal restriction on ticket prices. If the airline had sold 124 tickets, it could lower its price to sell the remaining ticket without having to lower the price for the remainder of the passengers. Once the plane took off, an empty seat represented foregone profit. In 1998, the *New York Times* reported that 27 different fares were charged to 33 customers on the same plane flying from Chicago to Los Angeles. The prices ranged from a low of $87.21 to a high of $1,248.51.[5]

In a *New York Times Magazine* article, Laurence Zuckerman explained how the airlines accomplished such a feat, more commonly referred to as **yield management**. Armed with sophisticated statistical software, computers review historical bookings, cancellations, and fares to determine how many tickets to release for sale, and at what price. Zuckerman broke yield management for an American Airlines flight from Phoenix to Dallas-Fort Worth into the following stages:

1. Six months prior to departure: The computer organizes the airfares into several categories, each with a different price. The number of discounted seats available for sale is limited to allow sales to last-minute premium buyers.

2. 48 days prior to departure: By now, 41 seats have been reserved for sale at steep discounts. Agents have been authorized to sell 154 seats, which exceeds capacity by 29 seats. No reservations have been taken in first class.

3. 13 days prior to departure: 21- and 14-day advance ticket sales have been closed. One-hundred-and-one seats have been booked. Airfares to Dallas have risen from $220/roundtrip to $448/roundtrip. Agents are authorized to overbook by 21 seats. There are still no reservations for first class.

4. Four hours prior to departure: The price of a roundtrip ticket is up to $1,142. Although the flight is already overbooked by 11 passengers, the agents are authorized to book three more tickets. The first-class cabin is now filled, largely by frequent flier passengers.

5. Five minutes before departure: The flight is overbooked by 13 passengers, but three took an earlier flight and the remainder is composed of no-shows, resulting in a full plane.

The final tally of paying customers is as follows:

1. 52 passengers purchased 21-day or 14-day advance tickets at prices between $220 and $420
2. 25 passengers purchased tickets with seven-day discounts
3. 35 passengers paid full fare for their tickets
4. 13 redeemed frequent flier credits
5. 2 passengers paid full fare for first-class seats
6. 12 passengers redeemed frequent flier tickets to obtain first-class seats.

Another industry that routinely implements yield management is the hotel industry. Hotels face a market that is quite similar to the airline industry. Like the airline, the number of rooms available for rent is pre-existing. Also similar to the airline, the marginal cost of filling a room for the night is quite small (washing towels, replacing soap, etc.). Consequently, it's better for the hotel to fill each room than it is to leave a few empty. If first-degree price discrimination was not possible, the hotel would determine the profit-maximizing price, which would likely lead to empty rooms. But if they can rent out rooms at discounted rates, while still renting other rooms at higher rates, they can add to their profits.

Priceline and HotWire are firms that assist hotels in price discriminating. Both firms use "opaque" models through which hotels can dump unsold rooms at discount prices without sacrificing revenues from their advertised retail prices. The firms negotiate with brand-name hotels for unlisted discount prices. Buyers, without knowing the names of the hotels, bid prices based on location and hotel class. If the bid price matches or exceeds the unlisted discount, the consumer is charged for the room at the bid price.

Does yield management work? American Airlines and Delta Airlines credit yield management with adding $500 million and $300 million per year, respectively, to their revenues.[6] Marriott attributes $100 million per year in revenues to yield management techniques.[7]

What does it take to make first-degree price discrimination work? Can anyone do it? To begin with, we need to recognize that extracting all consumer surplus is very difficult. Take the car salesman's attempt to price discriminate. His goal is to extract all that the prospective buyer is willing to pay to get the car. But he doesn't know what the person is willing to pay, and it behooves the buyer not to disclose the figure. The car dealer may succeed in obtaining some of the surplus, and maybe even all of it, but given that consumers have a vested incentive in concealing their willingness to pay, it would be very difficult for the dealer to extract the entire surplus from every consumer. Hence, the scenario depicted in Figure 5.3 represents perfect price discrimination. In real-world situations, firms that implement price discrimination strategies do so imperfectly; they are able to extract some, but not all consumer surplus.

Beyond that clarification, when is first-degree price discrimination most likely to work? Going back to Wendy's interior design business, one reason she was in a position to price discriminate was because clients with a lower willingness to pay were not able to purchase her work and re-sell it to clients with a greater willingness to pay. Suppose Wendy sold artwork rather than interior design. As with the interior design business, she has the ability to choose how many paintings she wants to sell, and she believes she can negotiate a price with each customer. Assume Dave is willing to pay as much as $5,000 for a painting, whereas Paul is not willing to pay more than $200. According to theory, Wendy charges Dave and Paul $5,000 and $200 for their paintings, respectively. But what if Paul buys his painting for $200 and then offers it to Dave for $4,000? For price discrimination to work, Wendy has to come up with a way to keep Paul from buying her work for a low price and re-selling it at a higher price. Obviously, this is not an issue for her interior design business. If she fixed up Paul's living room, he's not in a position to sell it to Dave.

For price discrimination to succeed, firms must subvert the potential for re-sale. This is not nearly as difficult as one might think. An athletic department at a major university, for example, may offer discount prices to students, based on the assumption that students have less income and, hence, a lower willingness to pay than working adults. In this scenario, the potential for re-sale is obvious: the students buy up a few hundred discounted tickets and then sell them at prices that are less than the face value of the regular tickets. With the Internet, creating efficient re-sale markets is comparatively easy. How do athletic departments keep this from happening? First, students often are required to buy their tickets in person. In this manner, the university can assure that only students who present their college IDs can purchase a ticket. To subvert the possibility of re-sale, each student ticket is often printed with a "Student Ticket" label. If a 40-year old shows up at the gate with a "Student Ticket," the ticket-taker is in a position to demand to see proof that the individual is, indeed, a college student.

Savvy readers may have noticed something about the dynamics of price discrimination. When an airline or hotel implements yield management, it does so by pricing the buyer with a lesser willingness to pay into the market without having to lower the price for the buyers with a greater willingness to pay. That's why it's a smart idea for the airline to sell every seat and for the hotel to rent out every room. But in most industries, the firm does not need to lower the price to suit the low-demand buyer; it can simply store the inventory to sell another day and exclude the low-demand buyer entirely. But the plane cannot store unused seats in inventory and sell them another day. Neither can the hotel do the same with its empty rooms. Once the plane takes off, the empty seat represents revenue foregone. Likewise, once dawn breaks the following day, an empty hotel room is a room that could have had a paying customer. For this reason, price discrimination works best when the product is perishable and cannot be stored to re-sell another day.

There is another common bond among the airline and hotel industries. In both cases, variable costs are negligible. Filling a seat or hotel room brings in revenue while having little or no impact on costs. Price discrimination can be successfully practiced when variable costs are higher. However, given that the goal is to price the more price sensitive buyers into the market, the firm has significantly more pricing flexibility when unit costs are low.

Summary

- First-degree price discrimination is the practice of charging each customer the maximum he is willing to pay.
- Successful first-degree price discrimination allows the firm to extract all of the consumer's surplus, thereby maximizing revenues.
- It is difficult to extract all consumer surplus because consumers have an incentive to disguise their willingness to pay.
- Because the firm does not have to charge the same price to all customers, the firm will maximize profits by producing each unit that can be sold at a price above its marginal cost. This will allow the firm to profitably sell more units than it would under a single price strategy.
- To successfully price discriminate, the firm must have some degree of market power and limit the ability of customers to re-sell the units at a higher price.
- First-degree price discrimination is often referred to as yield management and is widely practiced by airline and hotel rooms because variable costs are minimal and each seat/room that sits empty represents lost revenue that cannot be stored in inventory and re-sold on another day.

CHAPTER 6

Allowing Buyers to Self-Select By Willingness to Pay: Second-Degree Price Discrimination Strategies

Quantity Discounts

The obvious limitation of first-degree price discrimination is the level of consumer-specific information needed to extract the buyer's consumer surplus. An alternative to first-degree price discrimination is **second-degree price discrimination**. Here, the firm has an awareness of the distribution of consumer preferences in aggregate and a sense that different market segments exist. The goal of second-degree price discrimination, therefore, is to design a pricing scheme that causes buyers to self-select based on their willingness to pay. In doing so, the firm is able to extract some, albeit probably not all, of the buyers' consumer surplus.

One form of second-degree price discrimination is quantity discounts. This pricing practice implicitly recognizes the law of diminishing marginal utility. According to the law, each additional unit provides the consumer will less additional satisfaction. Therefore, the consumer's willingness to pay decreases with each successive unit.

To illustrate, Disney World allows patrons to buy tickets to any of its four Florida theme parks at a price of $85. Suppose each visit provides less additional utility. Let us assume that Marsha's willingness to pay for each park visit is indicated in Table 6.1. If Marsha's demand schedule is typical, note that the revenue-maximizing price is $85. (We will assume all costs are fixed; this implies that the revenue-maximizing price is also the profit-maximizing price). At this price, Marsha will visit parks on two days, for revenues totaling $170. We can also calculate Marsha's consumer surplus under the single-price strategy as equal to $35.

Table 6.1. Pricing Parks Individually

Park visits	Willingness to pay $	Consumer surplus $
1st day	120	120 − 85 = 35
2nd day	85	85 − 85 = 0
3rd day	50	
4th day	30	

Marsha would not be willing to visit the park on the 3rd day because the value she places on the experience ($50) is less than the price ($85). But under the 2011 Disney pricing policy, Marsha can opt to visit parks on three days for a package price of $231.99, or an average of $77.33 per day. At first glance, one might conclude that this would not make a difference because the price of the third day still exceeds the value she places on the third day. But Disney is not charging $77.33 for each day; rather, it is offering a package of three days for a price of $231.99 (or an average of $77.33 per day). Is the package worthwhile? According to Table 6.2, Marsha values three days of park visits at $255, so the three-day package seems to be quite a good value. As a result, Marsha pays $231.99 instead of $170. With the three-day package, Marsha's consumer surplus is $255 − $231.99, or $23.01.

Why did the package induce Marsha to go for an extra day? Under a single pricing strategy, Marsha weighs the value of each individual visit against its price. She values the first day at $120, but only has to pay $85. Hence, the $35 in consumer surplus is uncaptured by Disney. Disney captures the entire consumer surplus on the second day, but cannot entice her to spend a third day at the parks because the value she derives from a third day is less than the price. Although the package deal is promoted at an average price of $77.33/day, Table 6.2 shows the actual ramifications of the package deal.

Table 6.2. Effects of Quantity Discounts

Park visits	Willingness to pay $	Price $	Consumer surplus $
1st day	120	120	120 − 120 = 0
2nd day	85	85	85 − 85 = 0
3rd day	50	26.99	50 − 26.99 = 23.01
Total:	255	231.99	23.01

The package deal effectively captures Marsha's consumer surplus for the first two days. The remaining expenditure ($26.99) is less than the price of a ticket for the third day, so Marsha sees the overall value of the three-day package as worth the price.

Figures 6.1 and 6.2 illustrate the quantity discount graphically. Under the single-price strategy, the revenue-maximizing price is $85.

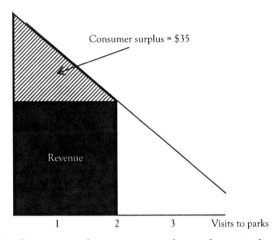

Figure 6.1. *Revenue and consumer surplus under a single-price strategy.*

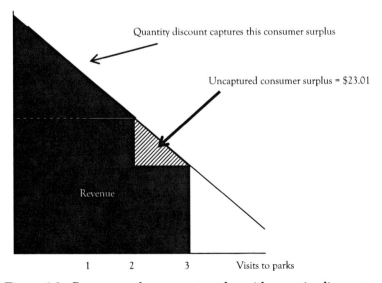

Figure 6.2. *Revenue and consumer surplus with quantity discounts.*

Marsha attends Disney parks on two days, with uncaptured consumer surplus totaling $35. Under the three-day package, Disney captures the consumer surplus from the first two visits, generates additional revenue from a third visit, while leaving uncaptured consumer surplus equal to $23.01.

But if the three-day package generates more revenue than the single-price strategy, why does Disney offer both? Let's create a slightly different demand schedule for Derek, another prospective visitor. Derek's willingness to pay is the same as Marsha's for every visit except the first. As indicated in Table 6.3, note that the revenue-maximizing price is still $85. Under the single-price strategy, Derek attends two parks, spends $170, with $5 in uncaptured consumer surplus. However, unlike Marsha, Derek's valuation of three visits is only $225, which is not sufficient to induce him to buy the $231.99 three-day package.

This example illustrates the benefits from offering the three-day package and the single pricing strategy simultaneously. Second degree price discrimination does not require the firm to know each person's demand schedule. Instead, it offers a pricing policy that allows consumers to self-select.

Table 6.3. Derek's Demand Schedule

Park visits	Willingness to pay $	Consumer surplus $
1st day	90	90 – 85 = 5
2nd day	85	85 – 85 = 0
3rd day	50	
4th day	30	

Frequent shopper programs are also a form of second-degree price discrimination. Here, the buyer gets credit for each purchase. Once the buyer accumulates sufficient credits, he gets his next order for free or for a significant discount.

Quality Choices

Another form of self-selection is to offer quality choices. In this case, the firm offers two different versions of the same product.

The higher priced version offers a higher quality product than the lower priced version. However, the profit margin on the higher priced version is greater than that on the lower quality version. This allows buyers to naturally self-select based on price sensitivity. Presumably, the more price sensitive consumers will choose the lower priced, lower quality version whereas the less price sensitive buyers will opt for the higher price, higher quality version.

Perhaps the most obvious example of quality choice-based price discrimination is first-class versus coach seats on an airplane. The cost of the seats to the airlines is nearly identical; the only real cost difference is the higher quality food and drinks available to first-class ticket buyers. The seats offer more elbow room and first-class patrons have the privilege of boarding and deplaning before the coach passengers, but these are perquisites that cost nothing to the airline, aside from the obvious opportunity cost of using up space that could go toward a few more paying customers. Of course, the opportunity cost is hardly nominal. If four first-class seats in a row replace six coach seats that would otherwise have been occupied, the airline must be able to charge a price that is at least 1.5 times higher than the price of a coach seat to make the venture worthwhile. Yet first-class seats are often 4–5 times higher than the price of an economy seat, thereby far exceeding the actual cost of servicing a first-class passenger relative to other passengers.

Similarly, Quicken offers a number of different products, from Quicken Starter Edition to Quicken Deluxe to Quicken Premier to Quicken Home and Business. Although the latter is priced three times higher than the Starter edition, it is higher unlikely that the cost of the Home and Business product is three times higher than the cost of producing the Starter edition.

We will use a numerical example to show how this works. Suppose a software company had but one standard version for which the marginal cost of each unit was $10. Market demand is illustrated in Table 6.4.

As the table indicates, the firm's profit contribution ($495) is maximized by charging a single price of $65.

Table 6.4. Profit-Maximizing with No Quality Choice

Price $	Quantity	Total variable cost $	Profit contribution $
100	1	10	90
85	5	50	375
65	9	90	495
45	13	130	455
25	16	160	$240

Suppose instead of a single, standard version, the firm manufactures two versions: the Starter version and the Deluxe version. The marginal costs are similar: each unit of the Starter version can be manufactured for $9 and each unit of the Deluxe version can be produced at a cost of $11. Market demand for each version at each price is shown in Table 6.5. (Note that the quantities demanded at each price sum to the totals shown in Table 6.4).

Table 6.5. Profit-Maximization with Quality Choices

Deluxe version				Starter version			
Price $	Quantity $	TVC $	Profit contri-bution $	Price $	Quantity $	TVC $	Profit contri-bution $
100	1	11	89	100	0	0	0
85	4	44	296	85	1	9	76
65	6	66	324	65	3	27	168
45	8	88	272	45	5	45	180
25	10	110	140	25	6	54	$96

As the table indicates, the profit-maximizing prices are $65 for the Deluxe version and $45 for the Starter version. By creating two versions, the firm's profit contribution rises from $495 to $504. The underlying assumption is that consumers will self-select to the product that reflects their willingness to pay.

Figure 6.3 illustrates the strategy. Rather than to charge the profit-maximizing price for the standard version, the firm produces two versions and prices them in accordance with the buyers' willingness to pay.

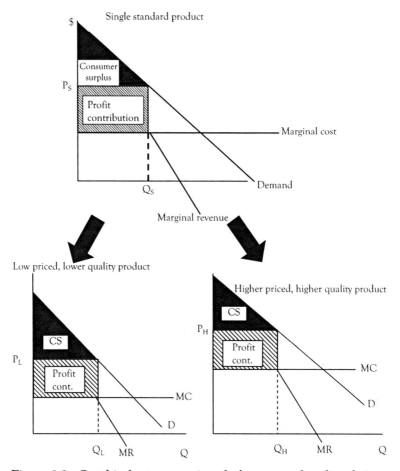

Figure 6.3. *Graphical representation of advantages of quality choices.*

Bundling

Pricing Individually Versus Pure Bundling

Another strategy that bears resemblance to quantity discounts and quality choices is **bundling**. Bundling exists when the firm offers multiple products as a "bundle" that differs from the sum of the prices of the two products purchased individually.[1] Bundling has become extremely popular in telecommunications. Customers may choose between mobile phone coverage, high-speed Internet service, and landline phone service, or some combination of the three at a price that is less than the sum of the individual prices.

The firm seeking to maximize profits can choose to either price its products individually, combine them into a bundle and offer only the bundle to customers (pure bundling), or offer the customers the choice of either the individual products or the bundle (mixed bundling). Our purpose is to determine which of these strategies is most profitable.

In the telecommunications industry, where bundling opportunities are widespread, the cost structure is heavily weighted toward fixed costs. Variable, or marginal costs, are minimal. Thus, to simplify the analysis, we will assume marginal costs are zero. If so, a firm that maximizes revenues will also maximize profits. We will later release this assumption. Suppose a telecommunications firm offers monthly mobile service, high-speed Internet, and landline phone service.

Assume we have three prospective customers: Archie, Byron, and Crystal. Table 6.6 shows their willingness to pay for each of the three products.

We will begin by assuming that the firm will price each product individually. According to the table, if mobile service is offered at a price of $100, only Archie will buy the service, generating $100 in revenue. If the firm charges $80 for mobile service, Archie and Byron will buy the service, which yields $160 in revenue. If the service is offered at a price of $70, all three consumers will purchase the service, which brings revenues totaling $210. Hence, the firm will charge $70 to maximize revenues.

The same analysis can be applied to the high-speed Internet and landline phone service (Table 6.7).

Table 6.6. Willingness to Pay for Unbundled Goods

	Archie $	Byron $	Crystal $
Mobile service	100	80	70
High-speed Internet	80	50	30
Landline phone	40	15	0

Table 6.7. Market Demands for Unbundled Goods

High-speed Internet			Landline phone service		
Price $	No. of customers $	Total revenue $	Price $	No. of customers $	Total revenue $
80	1	80	40	1	40
50	2	100	15	2	30
30	3	90	0	3	0

Pricing the three products individually will generate revenues equal to $350.

Suppose that instead of pricing the products individually, the firm offered only bundles. Table 6.6 shows that Archie would be willing to spend up to $220 for the bundle, Byron would be willing to spend $145, and Crystal would be willing to spend up to $100. Based on this information, Table 6.8 summarizes the firm's revenue if the bundle were to be priced at $220, $145, or $100.

As the table illustrates, revenues would be maximized by charging $100 for the bundle. Notice that the profit-maximizing bundle price generates only $300, whereas the sum of the profits from charging the individual profit-maximizing prices is $350. Thus, the firm would be more profitable offering each product separately instead of the bundle.

If we look at Table 6.6, we will see why. As the table exhibits, Archie values all three services more than either Byron or Crystal. Likewise, Byron values all three services more than Crystal. Because the relative valuation of the products does not differ across prospective customers, the firm cannot price a bundle that is more profitable than pricing each product individually.

Let's change the relative valuations between the three consumers and see how this affects the strategy. In Table 6.9, we changed the buyers' willingness to pay such that Archie values mobile service the most, Byron

Table 6.8. Market Demand for Bundle

Price $	No. of customers	Total revenue $
220	1	220
145	2	290
100	3	300

Table 6.9. Willingness to Pay when Relative Valuations Differ Across Consumers

	Archie $	Byron $	Crystal $
Mobile service	100	80	70
High-speed Internet	50	80	30
Landline phone	0	15	40

values high-speed Internet more than either Archie or Crystal, and Crystal exhibits the greatest willingness to pay for landline service.

Because we used the same willingness to pay figures (but attributed them to different consumers), the revenue-maximizing prices for separate mobile, Internet, and landline services are still $70, $50, and $40, respectively, and generate revenues of $210, $100, and $40, respectively. Thus, by pricing each product separately, the firm can earn a maximum of $350.

According to the figures in Table 6.9, Archie would be willing to spend up to $150 for the bundle, Byron would be willing to spend $175 on the bundle, and Crystal would spend up to $140 to obtain the bundle. Table 6.10 illustrates the revenue ramifications associated with bundle prices of $175, $150, and $140. As the Table indicates, charging $140 will yield revenues totaling $420.

Notice that the bundle is now more profitable than the maximum profit earned from pricing the goods separately. When the relative valuations did not differ between consumers (i.e. Archie was willing to pay the most for all three products and Byron was willing to pay the second most for all three goods), bundling did not increase the firm's revenue. However, when the relative valuation of the three goods differed between customers, bundling was a more profitable option than pricing each good separately.

Because a firm may potentially sell to many consumers, let's find a way to generalize the implications. To allow for a two-dimensional graph, we will limit the choices to mobile service and high-speed Internet. Suppose we have the following list of prospective customers for the two goods. The maximum price that each of 20 consumers is willing to pay for the respective goods, including the bundle (called the *reservation prices*) is shown in Table 6.11.

If we sort the prices from high to low, we can determine the revenue-maximizing price for each good, as shown in Table 6.12. The table shows

Table 6.10. *Market Demand for Bundle when Relative Valuations Differ Across Consumers*

Price $	No. of Customers	Total revenue $
175	1	175
150	2	300
140	3	420

Table 6.11. *Willingness to Pay for Bundled and Unbundled Goods Across Many Consumers*

Consumer	Reservation price for mobile service $	Reservation price for high-speed Internet $	Reservation price for bundle $
A	100	80	180
B	80	50	130
C	70	30	100
D	30	75	105
E	40	55	95
F	55	55	110
G	65	45	105
H	50	20	70
I	50	70	120
J	90	90	180
K	80	65	145
L	50	60	110
M	105	10	115
N	40	45	85
O	35	60	95

Table 6.12. *Market Demand for Unbundled Goods with Many Consumers*

Mobile service			High-speed Internet		
Price $	Quantity	Total revenue $	Price $	Quantity	Total revenue $
105	1	105	90	1	90
100	2	200	80	2	160
90	3	270	75	3	225
80	5	400	70	4	280
70	6	420	65	5	325
65	7	455	55	9	495
55	8	440	50	10	500
50	11	550	45	12	540
40	13	520	30	13	390
35	14	490	20	14	280
30	15	450	10	15	150

that the revenue-maximizing prices for mobile service and high-speed Internet are $50 and $45, respectively.

The scatterplot for the reservation prices appears in Figure 6.4. If we draw a line through the corresponding revenue-maximizing prices (the vertical line at $50 is the price of mobile service and the horizontal line at $45 is the price of Internet service), we can visualize the ramifications for pricing each good separately. If priced separately, consumers in quadrant I would buy only the high-speed Internet because their reservation price for high-speed Internet exceeds $45 whereas they would not be willing to pay $50 for mobile service. The opposite is true for consumers in quadrant IV. They would be willing to pay $50 or more for mobile service, but they would not be willing to pay $45 for high-speed Internet. Consumers whose reservation prices place them in quadrant II would buy both goods and persons in quadrant III would not purchase either product.

To see the implications for bundling, let's rank the reservation prices from high to low and determine the profit-maximizing bundle price (Table 6.13). As the table indicates, the revenue-maximizing bundle price is $95.

If we reproduce Figure 6.4 and draw a line through every combination of products whose prices sum to $95, we can visualize every consumer who would be willing to buy the bundle (Figure 6.5). Specifically, every consumer to the right of the bundle line would purchase the bundle

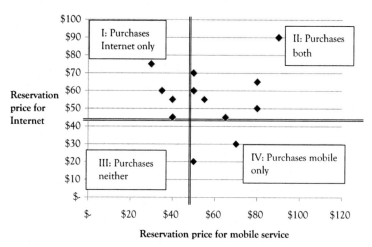

Figure 6.4. Reservation prices for unbundled goods.

Table 6.13. Market Demand for Bundle with Many Consumers

Price $	Quantity	Total revenue $
180	2	360
145	3	435
130	4	530
120	5	600
115	6	690
110	9	990
105	10	1050
100	11	1100
95	13	1235
85	14	1190
70	15	1050

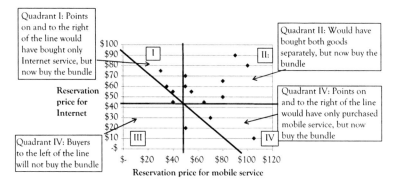

Figure 6.5. Potential buyers of a bundle.

at a price of $95. This can be readily seen by glancing back at Table 6.11. According to the table, only two consumers (H and N) would not be willing to pay $95 for the bundle. These two individuals are represented graphically as the two points that appear to the left of the $95-line.

Figure 6.5 allows us to see the impact of bundling. When the goods are priced separately, consumers in quadrant II buy both products whereas consumers in quadrants I and IV only purchase one of the two goods. By offering a bundle at the revenue-maximizing price of $95, all consumers in quadrant II buy the bundle, but this generates no additional revenue for the firm because they would have bought both services for a total of $95 anyway.[2]

However, if each product was priced separately, consumers in quadrants I and IV would have only purchased one of the two goods. Notice that by offering the bundle, the firm can induce five of these consumers to buy the bundle. For quadrant I, the difference between $95 and their willingness to pay for high-speed Internet is the increased revenue for the firm. For customers in quadrant IV, the increased revenue is represented by the difference between $95 and their willingness to pay for mobile service.

We can refer to Table 6.11 to see numerical examples. Consumer C is willing to spend $70 for mobile service and $30 for high-speed Internet. Priced separately at $50 and $45, respectively, consumer C will only buy the mobile service. But C values mobile service and high-speed Internet collectively at $100. Therefore, C is willing to pay $95 for the bundle. The firm collects $95 from C instead of $70. Consumer E values mobile service and high-speed Internet at $40 and $55, respectively. This individual (who appears in quadrant I in Figure 6.5) would only purchase high-speed Internet if the products were sold separately. But the bundle is worth $95 to him. Therefore, by offering the bundle, consumer E spends $95 for both services instead of $55 for high-speed Internet only.

Let's rearrange the reservation prices. This time, the same set of prices are rearranged (Table 6.14) such that consumer A is willing to pay the

Table 6.14. Willingness to Pay When Relative Valuations do not Vary

Consumer	Reservation price for mobile service $	Reservation price for high-speed Internet $	Reservation price for bundle $
A	105	90	195
B	100	80	180
C	90	75	165
D	80	70	150
E	80	65	145
F	70	60	130
G	65	60	125
H	55	55	110
I	50	55	110

(Continued)

Table 6.14. Willingness to Pay When Relative Valuations do not Vary—(Continued).

Consumer	Reservation price for mobile service $	Reservation price for high-speed Internet $	Reservation price for bundle $
J	50	50	100
K	50	45	95
L	40	45	85
M	40	30	70
N	35	20	55
O	30	10	40

most for both mobile service and high-speed Internet, consumer B is willing to pay the second-most for each product, and so on. Without reproducing the arithmetic, the revenue-maximizing prices for high-speed Internet, mobile service, and the bundle are the same as in the previous exercise.

The scatterplot exhibiting the reservation prices and the revenue-maximizing product/bundle prices appear in Figure 6.6. Note that the reservation prices follow a pattern that is upward-sloping. Note also that every consumer lies in either quadrant II or quadrant III. Thus, by offering the bundle, the firm sells to all of the consumers who would have bought both products anyway, but cannot entice anyone to buy the bundle who would have only purchased one service otherwise. We can see this by examining Table 6.14. Consumers A through K (depicted in quadrant II in Figure 6.6) would be willing to buy each product separately because each has a willingness to pay for mobile service and high-speed Internet that exceeds $50 and $45. Therefore, the firm would collect $95 from each of these customers if the services were priced separately. The same individuals will buy the bundle for $95. Hence, the firm collects no additional revenue from these individuals.

If we examine consumers L through M (depicted in quadrant III in Figure 6.6), we can see that none of them would be willing to pay $95 for the bundle. Thus, bundling the services does not entice anyone to buy more services collectively than if the products were available individually. Figure 6.5 revealed that the bundle enticed some individuals

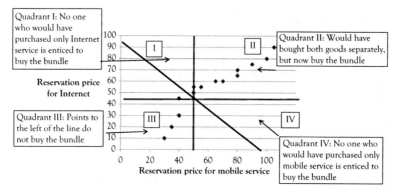

Figure 6.6. Plot of reservation prices when relative valuations do not vary.

(those in quadrants I and IV) who would have only purchased one of the services to buy the bundle. But Figure 6.6 reveals that there are no consumers in either of these quadrants.

Relating this to the "real-world" is easy. Suppose an individual is willing to spend up to $80 for mobile service, but no longer owns a landline. If a telecommunications firm offers mobile service for $75 and landline service for $30, the consumer will buy the mobile service because he places no value on landline service. Offer the bundle for a discounted price of $85 (less than the combined prices) without an opportunity to buy either one separately and the same consumer will not buy the bundle. By only offering the bundle, the firm loses $75.

Figures 6.5 and 6.6 help illustrate the ramifications for bundling. The lesser is the variation in relative valuations across prospective customers (i.e. the more highly correlated the rank order of preferences for each good), the lesser is the opportunity to gain by bundling. In contrast, the more negatively correlated the relative valuations across prospective customers (i.e. the person willing to pay the most for one good is willing to pay the least for the other good), the greater the potential gains from bundling.

Pure Bundling Versus Mixed Bundling

The previous analysis discussed the potential benefits of pricing a bundle rather than setting individual prices for each good. An alternative is to offer the consumer a choice of either the bundle or the individually priced goods (mixed bundle). Figure 6.5 shows the ramifications of mixed bundling. If only offered the bundle for $95, 13 consumers would make the purchase. Two consumers have bundle reservation prices below $95 (i.e. graphically, they lie to the left of the bundle line) and would not buy the bundle. However, one consumer values mobile service at a price of $50 and another values high-speed Internet at a price of $45. Thus, when offered the opportunity to either buy the bundle or an individual product, these two persons (consumers H and N from Table 6.14) would buy the mobile and Internet service, respectively, adding $95 to the firm's total revenue.

Thus far, we relied on an analysis in which all costs were assumed to be fixed; hence, the price that maximized revenues also maximized profit contribution. Let's return to the simple example of Archie, Byron, and Crystal to see the implications. Table 6.15 reproduces each person's set of reservation prices.

Let's assume the marginal cost of mobile service is $75, the marginal cost of high-speed Internet is $40, and the marginal cost of landline phone service is $10. The marginal costs were rigged such that at least one consumer has a reservation price that is below marginal cost. For example, Crystal is only willing to pay $70 for mobile service. Because the service carries a marginal cost of $75, the firm cannot fashion a price that would suit her. If we limit the choice of individual prices to the reservation prices that would generate a profit, we can see that the profit-maximizing mobile, Internet, and landline phone service prices are $100, $80, and $40, respectively, as shown in Table 6.16. At these prices, each consumer would buy exactly one product and the firm's total profits would be equal to $95.

The marginal cost of a bundle is the sum of the individual marginal costs, or $125. Using the sum of each person's reservation prices to indicate their willingness to pay for a bundle, we can see the price that will maximize profits.

Table 6.15. *Willingness to Pay When Value is Less than Marginal Cost for Some Customers*

	Archie $	Byron $	Crystal $
Mobile service	100	80	70
High-speed Internet	50	80	30
Landline phone	0	15	40

Table 6.16. Market Demand for Unbundled Goods

Mobile			Internet			Landline		
Price $	Qty	Profit contri- bution $	Price $	Qty	Profit contri- bution	Price $	Qty	Profit contri- bution $
100	1	25	80	1	40	40	1	30
80	2	10	50	2	20	15	2	10

Table 6.17. Market Demand for Bundle

Price $	Quantity	Profit contribution $
175	1	50
150	2	50
140	3	45

As Table 6.17 indicates, the bundle is less profitable than pricing the goods individually. However, suppose the firm offers the consumers a choice of either the bundle or the individual goods. If the bundle is priced at $175, Byron will buy the bundle, Archie will purchase mobile service for $100, and Crystal will buy landline service for $40. Collectively, the mixed bundling strategy will generate profit contribution equal to $105.[3]

As we apply theory to the real world, which bundling option is likely to be most profitable? As we noted, if the reservation prices across consumers are positively correlated, bundling will not be more profitable than individual pricing. Often, however, firms offer products that have substitutable traits. An individual with a high reservation price for mobile service is unlikely to have an equally high reservation price for landline phone service, as one tends to substitute for the other. Moreover, often the available products cater to individual tastes. Cable/satellite companies tend not to offer a la carte programming because their customers have varying tastes. One prospective customer is likely to place a high value on sports-related programming whereas another will prefer channels that offer programs on home improvement. Moreover, because the time available for watching television is fixed, an individual with a high preference for some types of programming must have a relatively low preference for other programming. Thus, in most cases in which bundling may be considered, it is unlikely that reservation prices for individual products are positively correlated.

The best opportunities for bundling occur as the reservation prices become increasingly negatively correlated. The notion of a perfect inverse correlation (the consumer who values one good the most values the other good the least) would seem rather unlikely. However, to the extent that a negative correlation between reservation prices is more likely than a positive correlation, bundling can be the more profitable alternative. In general, mixed bundling is best when individual prospective customers have reservation prices that are less than the marginal cost of the good. Again, this would seem to be a very likely scenario for most firms.

There are ample examples of bundling beyond choosing between mobile service, cable, and landline phone service. Cable/satellite companies usually offer mixed bundling alternatives. DirecTV, for example, offers several bundles (Choice, Choice Extra, Choice Ultimate, and Choice Premier). In addition to the bundles, subscribers can add individual paid channels such as HBO or a sports package such as NFL Sunday Ticket. Auto manufacturers also offer mixed bundling or pure bundling packages. Many manufacturers allow for mixed bundling in which several models of a car are available in which the standard equipment increases with various price levels. In addition to the models, consumers can add options that suit their preferences. Other manufacturers offer pure bundling alternatives by packaging the options as standard equipment. Fast food restaurants offer mixed bundles. Diners can pick and choose between individual menu items or they can buy a bundle (i.e. burger, fries, and a drink) for a price that is less than the sum of the individual menu prices. Note that the bundled menu items offer larger portions than the individually priced items. Although McDonald's offers small drinks and fries as individual menu items, the Extra Value Meals only offer medium or large drinks and fries.

Tying

Related to bundling is the concept of *tying*. Tying occurs when the seller requires the buyer to purchase a different product. The difference between bundling and tying is that, with the former, the consumer can obtain enjoyment through the purchase of only one good. For example, the buyer of mobile service can enjoy the benefits of a cell phone without purchasing landline service. In the case of tying, the consumer cannot obtain the benefits of the first good without the benefits of the second good.

Many tying requirements have been pronounced an illegal restraint of trade by the Supreme Court. The monopolist's incentive to tie purchases together was established in the *IBM v. United States* court case. IBM required entities that leased their mainframe computers to also buy the paper cards used by the machines by IBM. Although IBM had no direct information on the lessee's willingness to pay, it extracted consumer surplus indirectly by charging relatively high prices for its cards. Hence, the greater the willingness to pay (based on machine usage), the more the lessee paid.

Another example of illegal tying was block booking by movie studios. This practice required exhibitors to purchase a below-quality film they did not want in order to buy the movie they did want. The practice was deemed illegal twice: once in 1948 (United States v. Paramount Pictures, Inc.) and again in 1962 (United States v. Loew's, Inc.).

Allegations of illegal tying were also made when Apple released the iPhone in 2007. The iPhone was sold through exclusive contracts with AT&T. The iPhone came with a special software lock that made it inoperable with any other carrier than AT&T. If the buyer wanted to use the iPhone with another carrier, the individual had to pay a $175 termination fee to unlock the software.

Legal tying can exist when manufacturers create a product that requires a manufacturer-specific complementary good. As an example, in 2011, Dell Computers offered its V515w printer at a price of $74.99. However, it requires model-specific color and black ink cartridge replacements that retail for $19.99 and $15.99, respectively. Consequently, the consumer will pay for the equivalent of a new printer after only two refills.

Similarly, the Gillette web site revealed that its Fusion Power razor could be purchased online from WalMart for $9.47. The Fusion Power requires its own product-specific razor blades. According to the WalMart website, an eight-pack of replacement blades cost $29.57, roughly three times as much as the razor itself. In Chapter 2, we noted the relationship between the price of one good and the demand for a complementary good. By lowering the price of one good, the demand for its complement increases.

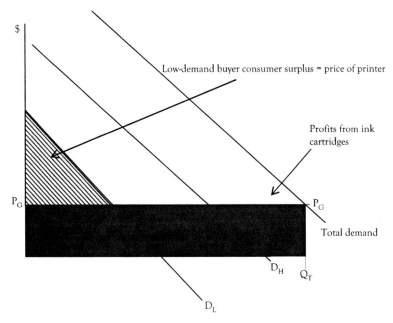

Figure 6.7. Graphical representation of tying.

The economic advantages of tying can be illustrated graphically. Suppose we have two types of computer printer users: one who prints extensively and one who prints occasionally. Figure 6.7 shows the ink cartridge demand schedules for the light user (D_L) and the heavy user (D_H). Assume the printer manufacturer is considering producing a printer that can use any generic ink cartridge that can be sold at the market price P_G. Because the printer is worthless without ink cartridges, the highest price the firm can charge for a printer and still attract both customers is equal to the consumer surplus of the light user. Let's take a moment to explain why this is true. At the inkjet price of P_G, each buyer's consumer surplus represents the uncaptured value from printing. The consumer surplus of the heavy user will necessarily be greater than that of the light user. If the price of a printer is less than the consumer surplus of the light user, both consumers will buy the printer, print the number of copies that corresponds to P_G (which will be greater for the heavy user) and still have uncaptured consumer surplus. If the price of the printer exceeds the light user's consumer surplus, the light user will not buy the printer at all because the price exceeds the surplus value that he places on printing. But even if the light user doesn't buy the printer, the heavy user will purchase it as long as the printer price is less than his consumer surplus. Therefore, if the price of the printer exceeds the consumer surplus of the light user, all of the profits will come from the heavy user. If the price of the printer is set equal to the light user's consumer surplus, both consumers will buy the printer and all of the light buyer's consumer surplus will be captured.

If we assume that both users will purchase the manufacturer's own ink cartridges as long as the price is competitive with the other generic producers, the firm's total profit will be double the low-demand buyer's consumer surplus (both the heavy and light user buy the printer) plus the profits from the ink cartridges (graphically, it is represented by the dark area between the generic price of ink cartridges and the total quantity of ink cartridges purchased by the heavy and light user at that price (Q_T).

Now let us change the printer to allow for tying. The implicit assumption is that the firm will be able to charge a higher price for the ink cartridges (P_I) because they cannot be substituted by generic brands. Figure 6.8 shows the implications. Note that the higher price of ink cartridges reduces the consumer surplus of the light user. This implies that the firm will have to lower the price of the printer to entice both consumers to buy the printer.

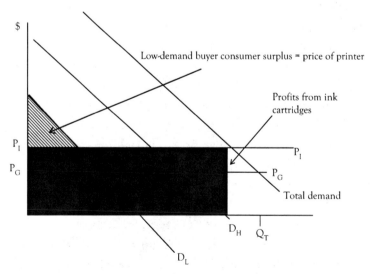

Figure 6.8. Implications from raising the price of the complementary good.

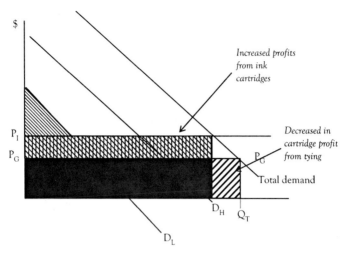

Figure 6.9. Net benefits from tying.

Figure 6.9 allows one to see the net benefits from tying. The light shaded area shows the increased profit contribution from charging a higher price for the model-specific ink cartridges. The striped area shows the reduction in profit contribution because the higher priced ink cartridges give the user an incentive to reduce printer consumption. Note that the reduction in printer price is more than offset by the increased profit contribution from the model-specific ink cartridges. Therefore, as the figure illustrates, tying is more profitable as long as the light shaded area (the increased profits from the model-specific ink cartridges) exceed the striped area (the lost profits from deterring usage due to more expensive ink cartridges).

Two-Part Tariffs

A **two-part tariff** exists when the buyer is required to pay an upfront fee to purchase the product and subsequent fees for each unit consumed. As we will see, the analysis bears a great deal of similarity to tying. Consider, for example, a state fair. Typically, the patron pays an entrance fee, but must pay additional fees for each ride or concession. Examples of two-part tariffs abound. Country clubs charge membership fees while charging additional fee for each round of golf or use of the tennis courts.

Professional sports franchises often require fans to purchase a personal seat license (often for thousands of dollars) for the right to purchase season tickets. Costco and Sam's Club require patrons to pay a membership fee as a condition to shop at their stores. Cell phone services also employ two-part tariffs. Subscribers pay a monthly base fee, which allows a fixed number of minutes, text messages, etc., and then pay additional fees for each minute or text message over that allotment.

The theory underlying the two-part tariff is fairly simple. Suppose we have a large number of consumers with identical tastes. The law of diminishing marginal utility creates a downward-sloping demand curve, such as that which is illustrated in Figure 6.10. The figure depicts the profit-maximizing price and quantity and the level of consumer surplus. The entry fee is set equal to the level of consumer surplus. Note that because the entry fee is a sunk cost, and is equal to consumer surplus, it has no impact on the number of units purchased.

Of course, consumers are unlikely to have identical tastes. To expand theory to allow for differing tastes, assume we have two consumers: one with a high demand for the good and another with a low demand (similar to what we did with tying). This is depicted in Figure 6.11. Note that the consumer surplus for the high-demand buyer will be larger at any given price than that of the low-demand buyer. If the usage fee was set equal to

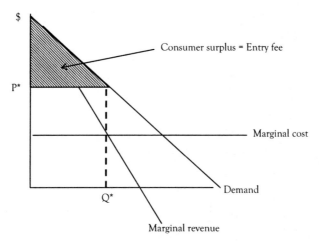

Figure 6.10. Two-part tariff: one customer.

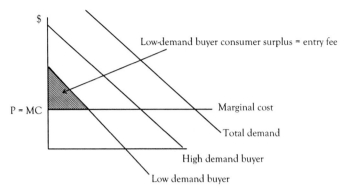

Figure 6.11. Two-part tariff: high- and low-demand customer.

marginal cost and the entry fee was equal to the consumer surplus of the high-demand buyer, the low-demand buyer would not pay the entry fee. On the other hand, if the entry fee was equal to the consumer surplus of the low-demand buyer, both the low- and the high-demand buyer would pay the entry fee. Hence, the entry fee revenues would be equal to twice the size of the low-demand buyer's consumer surplus shown in Figure 6.11.

Figure 6.11 does not, however, depict the entry and usage fees that will maximize profits. By setting the usage price equal to marginal cost, the firm only profits from the entry fees. If the firm raises its price above marginal cost while keeping the entry fee the same, the low demand buyer will not purchase the entry fee (because its consumer surplus at the usage price is now less than the entry fee, as shown in Figure 6.12).

If the firm was to charge a usage fee equal to P_1 and an entry fee equal to the consumer surplus of the low-demand buyer, the total profit would be twice the entry fee (paid by both consumers) and the shaded area between the price and marginal cost for all Q_T units consumed (the usage profit contribution from the high- and low-demand buyers).

The implications from the two-consumer illustration can be extrapolated to many consumers. From the decision-maker's perspective, the notion that a firm has sufficient information to replicate the fees shown in Figure 6.12 is unrealistic. The figure does, however, illuminate the trade-offs inherent in two-part tariffs. First, as the entry fee becomes larger, the number of entrants decreases. This causes the firm to lose out on the usage profit contribution from each excluded patron. Raising the usage price

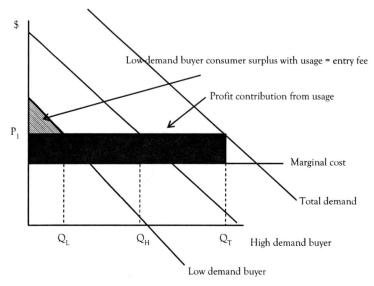

Figure 6.12. Two-part tariff trade-off between entry fee and price of goods.

increases the profit contribution from each patron, but it also necessitates lowering the entry fee to avoid losing customers.

To illustrate, consider a movie theater. The movie theater generates profits from two sources: ticket purchases and concessions sales. Therefore, the theater owner has to determine two sets of prices: one for ticket prices and another for concessions. In setting the corresponding prices, the owner knows that whereas all concessions customers will buy movie tickets, not all ticket buyers will purchase concessions. Moreover, no one buys a movie ticket simply to gain access to the concessions. From this perspective, it would make no sense to offer cheap concessions and high ticket prices. Instead, the owner has an incentive to hold ticket prices down to increase the number of prospective concessions customers, and then to raise concessions prices as a way to segment the buyers.

Implementing a two-part tariff does not come without costs. Prior to 1980, Disney theme parks offered a "passport" that included admission and a predetermined number of rides. Tickets for additional rides could be purchased at five different price tiers; the more popular the ride, the higher the price. Because the cost of administering the system was

ALLOWING BUYERS TO SELF-SELECT BY WILLINGNESS TO PAY

relatively high, the two-part tariff was discarded in favor of the simpler single admission fee policy in 1980.

Intertemporal Price Discrimination

Intertemporal price discrimination is the practice of charging different prices at different points in time as a means of reaching different market segments. In marketing literature, it is associated with price skimming. The strategy is widely practiced in electronics. When a new gadget hits the marketplace, some consumers, anxious to be the "first guy on the block" to own one, are willing to pay a relatively high price for the good. Once this segment of the market has been saturated, the firm lowers the price to attract the more price sensitive customers.

Many years ago, the movie theater industry was composed of first- and second-run movie houses. The first-run movie houses featured the latest films at higher prices. Once the movies had made their run at the first-run theaters, they would disappear briefly and then reappear at the second-run movie houses at discount prices. Nowadays, the market segment served by second-run movie houses has largely been replaced by the movie rental market. Consumers who were unwilling to pay the first-run prices are able to download or rent the same films several months later at lower prices.

From a theoretical perspective, here is how intertemporal price discrimination works. The firm realizes that it has two market segments that vary by price sensitivity. The firm cannot identify the market segments directly, but can use price skimming to allow them to self-select. Figure 6.13 shows the two market segments: the demand curve on the left (D_{Now}) is the less price sensitive group that is willing to pay a higher price to get the good soon after it becomes available. The demand curve on the right (D_{Later}) is more price sensitive that is willing to defer buying the good until the price is right. To capitalize on the two segments, the firm sets the profit-maximizing price and quantity for the less price sensitive segment and then, at a later date, the firm lowers the price to attract the more price sensitive segment.

Although the timing of price decreases is rarely the subject of controversy, Apple drew the ire of its customer base when the iPhone was first

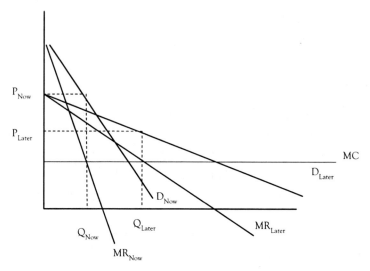

Figure 6.13. Graphical representation of price skimming.

introduced. The iPhone was released to much fanfare in September 2007. It was priced at $599. Only 69 days later, Apple dropped the price by $200. The early adopters were enraged by the rapid and significant price decrease, causing Apple CEO Steve Jobs to offer a $100 store credit to early adopters.

In addition to the risks of alienating the customer base by cutting prices too quickly, the firm has to consider the response of potential rivals. By setting its prices relatively high initially, the firm enjoys greater profits. However, in doing so, it invites competition to create a lower priced alternative. For this reason, some firms forego the skimming strategy in favor of a penetration pricing strategy. In this case, the firm enters the market with the price that seeks to maximize long-term profits. Here, the firm may even set a price that is below marginal cost and then raise it later on. The assumption is that the firm can reach a broad customer base immediately, and ideally, establish brand loyalty before rival firms enter the market.

Microsoft used a penetration strategy when it introduced its Windows Live OneCare antivirus package in 2006. With an average price below $30, the package vaulted to #2 in terms of market share in its debut month.[4]

The penetration strategy is illustrated in Figure 6.14. The firm hopes to penetrate the market quickly by its introductory price that is below marginal cost (P_{Now}). By creating a customer base quickly, the firm hopes to instill brand loyalty, which will cause the demand for the firm's good to increase in the future (D_{Later}). After demand increases, the firm can increase the price to its long-run profit-maximizing level (P_{Later}).

The penetration strategy works best when the firm is producing a good that is repurchased frequently. The assumption is that by establishing a sense of brand loyalty, the consumer will continue to purchase the product in the future. The strategy is most suitable when product demand is relatively elastic. The market should be large enough that the firm can effectively supply a large number of buyers at the introductory price. The strategy is particularly useful if significant ***economies of scale*** exist in production. Economies of scale occur when unit costs decrease over the long haul as production increases. Hence, by pricing low, unit sales are sufficiently large that the firm can profitably produce at a relatively low unit cost.

Firms should be wary of the possible consequences of the penetration strategy. Although the purpose is to attract buyers early on and establish

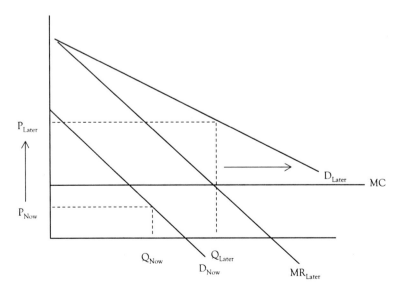

Figure 6.14. Graphical representation of penetration pricing.

brand loyalty, the plan could backfire if its only effect is to draw price sensitive buyers who will switch to another brand as soon as the price rises. This implies that firms choosing this strategy should work to develop product-specific attributes to keep their customers once they attract them.

Peak-Load Pricing

Peak-load pricing refers to the practice of setting different prices for "peak" and "off-peak" periods of demand. The purpose of peak-load pricing is to redistribute demand. Prior to the proliferation of cell phones, consumers may recall that the rates charged for long-distance phone calls were significantly cheaper after 11 PM. The telephone companies' switching capacity (i.e. its ability to connect one caller to another) is fixed, but phone usage tends to be greatest during the day. Thus, the marginal cost of providing phone service is high during peak periods but is much lower during off-peak hours when much of the switching capacity goes unused. By charging a lower rate for off-peak usage, the phone company redistributes demand away from peak usage toward nonpeak usage.

Figure 6.15 provides a graphical illustration of peak-load pricing. The figure shows two levels of demand: peak demand (D_p) and off-peak demand (D_O). The upward-sloping marginal cost curve corresponds to the firm's higher variable costs during peak usage. As opposed to setting a single profit-maximizing price, the firm sets two separate prices that correspond to peak (P_p) and off-peak demand (P_O).

Hotels and resorts deal with peak- and off-peak demand in a similar fashion. As with the telephone industry, capacity is fixed over the short-term and cannot be increased quickly. Therefore, if hotel rates never changed, the hotel may find itself turning away customers during periods of peak demand while exhibiting low occupancy rates during off-peak periods. An individual hoping to check into the Portofino Bay Hotel outside the Universal Studios resort during the week of Christmas would pay $404/night. Three weeks later, when children return to school and the resort is well into its off-peak period, the same room could be booked for only $279/night.[5]

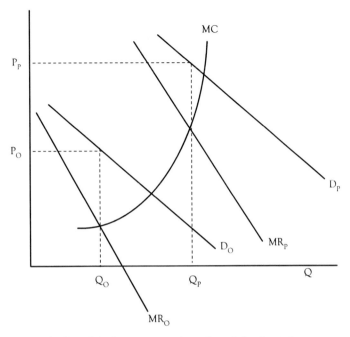

Figure 6.15. Graphical representation of peak-load pricing.

London developed an innovative peak-load pricing system to deal with congestion in its central business district in 2003. Private vehicles in London's central district between 7 AM and 6:30 PM on weekdays must pay an £8 congestion fee. A network of video cameras records the license plates of vehicles and imposes a fine of £80 to those who have not paid the congestion fee. Roughly 110,000 drivers per day pay the fee. After the fee was introduced, the percentage of private vehicle traffic flowing into the central district declined by 20%, or by 20,000 vehicles. As a result, congestion delays decreased by 30%, while bus ridership and subway usage increased by 14% and 1%, respectively.[6]

Summary

- Second degree price discrimination is the practice of offering pricing alternatives that cause buyers to self-select based on their willingness to pay.

- Quantity discounts exploit the law of diminishing marginal utility by creating a package that entices the consumer to buy more than he would have otherwise.
- Quality choices allow the buyer to self-select according to quality, as with the choice between first-class or coach seats on a plane.
- Bundling will be more profitable than pricing goods separately if the relative valuations of prospective consumers differ. Because consumer tastes tend to vary between goods (John is willing to pay more for mobile service than Mary, but Mary is willing to pay more for landline service than John), bundling will generally be more profitable than pricing goods separately.
- Mixed bundling, which refers to offering consumers the option of either the bundle or the individual goods, will be more profitable than pure bundling when some consumers' willingness to pay is less than the unit cost of one of the goods. Requiring a consumer to buy a bundle when he has minimal interest in buying one of the goods may cause him not to buy at all.
- Tying can increase profits by enticing the consumer to buy one good at a relatively low price, and making up for it with a higher price margin on the complementary good. Examples include razors/razor blades and printers/ink cartridges.
- A two-part tariff involves an entry fee and a separate usage fee. An example would be a fair that charges an admission fee and separate prices for rides and concessions. Because the firm does not want to price the more price sensitive consumer out of paying for admission, two-part tariffs involve a trade-off between the admission fee and the usage fee. In general, the higher the usage fee, the lower the admission fee.
- Intertemporal price discrimination refers to charging different prices at different points in time. Price skimming refers to introducing a good at a relatively high price to attract consumers who want to be "the first one on the block" to own one. Once this market is tapped, the firm lowers the price

to attract the more price sensitive buyer. In a penetration strategy, the firm starts with a low price to attract customers and build brand loyalty, only to raise the price later on. The benefit of the penetration strategy is that it makes it harder for competition to enter the market due to the low price. The potential disadvantage is that the low price will attract price sensitive buyers who will leave once the price rises.

• Peak load pricing is charging different prices to redistribute demand. It is useful if the alternative is to incur significant costs to meet demand during peak periods.

CHAPTER 7

Segmenting Your Market Based on Willingness to Pay: Third-Degree Price Discrimination Strategies

Third-degree price discrimination exists when different prices are charged to individuals who can be grouped according to their characteristics. The assumption is that price sensitivity and willingness to pay might differ across groups of individuals with readily identifiable characteristics. Examples of third-degree price discrimination include senior citizen discounts, discounts for children, etc. The key distinction between second- and third-degree price discrimination is that, in the former, the market segments cannot be recognized ex ante. Hence, the firm creates a pricing structure that allows buyers to self-select. In contrast, the firm has some ability to distinguish willingness to pay before-the-fact, and therefore, sets its prices based on the inferred willingness to pay for each market segment.

To illustrate, a college athletic department knows that some of its football fan base is made up of rabid fans whose life revolves around the football program. Other fans are interested in football and are willing to pay to go to the games, but may have a lower willingness to pay. Unfortunately, the department has no way to discern the rabid fan from the fair-weather fan. Suppose, for example, the department infers that rabid fans are willing to pay $50/ticket but fair-weather fans are not willing to pay more than $30. Moreover, rabid fans can be counted on to attend every game regardless of the weather or win–loss record of the team whereas the fair-weather fans are not likely to buy tickets if the weather is bad or if the team is having a bad season. Suppose the athletic department attempts to discriminate between the groups by offering season tickets for $300 (or $50/ticket) and individual tickets for $30. The athletic director theorizes that fair-weather fans would not be willing to buy a set of season tickets at $30/game because they prefer to make purchase decisions one game at a time. Rabid fans, on the other hand, will always choose to attend every game and have a greater willingness to pay.

If the athletic department attempts to implement this pricing strategy based on its inferences on the two groups' willingness to pay, it will likely fail. Even though the rabid group may be willing to pay $300 for season tickets, it can opt for six $30 tickets instead and save $120 in doing so. The problem is that, even though the athletic department may be correct in its inferences regarding willingness to pay between rabid and fair-weather fans, it cannot discern who belongs to which group before-the-fact.

On the other hand, suppose the athletic department assumes that its students, due to their lower incomes, have a lower willingness to pay relative to its nonstudent fan base. To illustrate the distinction, examine the demand schedule in Table 7.1. The demand schedule does not distinguish the students from the nonstudents. Assuming the marginal cost of a seat is equal to zero, the department will maximize revenues by charging a price of $75 and earning revenues of $3,525,000 million per game.

Suppose, however, the market demand schedule illustrated in Table 7.1 can be broken down into students and nonstudents. Assume the students have a lower willingness to pay. The corresponding demand schedules are shown in Table 7.2.

Note that at the revenue-maximizing price of $75 only 2,000 students will buy tickets. Suppose the athletic department decided to establish two ticket prices: one for student and the other for nonstudents. Under the

Table 7.1. Overall Demand for Tickets

Price $	Quantity	Revenues $
100	31,000	3,100,000
75	47,000	3,525,000
50	58,000	2,900,000
25	72,500	1,812,500
10	90,000	900,000

Table 7.2. Segmented Demand for Tickets

Students			Nonstudents		
Price $	Quantity	Revenues $	Price $	Quantity	Revenues $
100	1,000	100,000	100	30,000	3,000,000
75	2,000	150,000	75	45,000	3,375,000
50	3,000	150,000	50	55,000	2,750,000
25	7,500	187,500	25	65,000	1,625,000
10	15,000	150,000	10	75,000	750,000

two-tiered pricing scheme, nonstudents would continue to pay $75, but student tickets would be priced at $25. By setting a lower price for the more price-sensitive group, the athletic department is able to increase its revenues by $37,500. The solution is illustrated in Figure 7.1. As the figure indicates, by separating the overall market into two market segments based on price elasticity, the more price-sensitive group pays a lower price than the less price-sensitive segment, causing overall revenues to rise.

Earlier, we noted the importance of preempting opportunities for consumers to resell the good. We can revisit that concept in the context of third-degree price discrimination. To assure the more price elastic group does not re-sell the good, the firm has to be somewhat creative. In the case of the student tickets, the athletic department can create tickets with the words "Student Ticket" or a ticket with a different color. In that fashion, enforcement at the gate will come easier: if a 40-year old man shows up at the gate with a "student ticket," the attendant can ask to see a student ID.

Groupon combines elements of both second and third-degree price discrimination. Groupon offers daily group/coupons in its markets. If enough people sign up for the discount, they all receive it; otherwise, no one gets the deal. From the retailers' perspective, Groupon represents a convenient vehicle for third-degree price discrimination. By subscribing, consumers label themselves as price-sensitive and are offered a discounted price relative to nonsubscribers. From Groupon's perspective, its business model is one of second-degree price discrimination. Rather than to identify price sensitive customers based on demographic characteristics, it simply allows consumers to self-select: those are relatively price sensitive subscribe to the service whereas less price sensitive consumers do not.

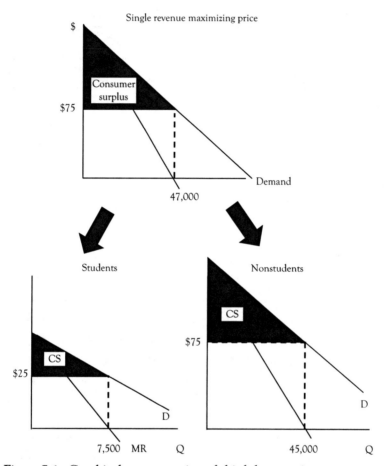

Figure 7.1. Graphical representation of third-degree price discrimination.

The Groupon business model also limits arbitrage possibilities. First, subscribers must prepay for the discount. Second, they must agree to the limitations of the offer (i.e. limit one per person). Third, the discounted deals have expiration dates. Groupon Now deals, for example, must be used within 24 hours. Note how the three elements combine to minimize re-selling. By prepaying, the subscriber incurs risk: if he is unable to find someone to re-sell the product or service, he suffers a loss. The limitations of the deal and the expiration dates make it more difficult for the subscriber to re-sell the deal at a profit.

Summary

- Third degree price discrimination exists when firms divide customers into groups based on their price sensitivity and charge separate prices to each group. Examples include senior citizen discounts and discounted prices for children.
- For third degree price discrimination to succeed, the firm must be able to readily identify each group and be capable of subverting opportunities for buyers to purchase the good and resell it.

PART III

How Does My E-Tailer Know that I Read Comic Books and Cook with a Wok? Pricing in the Digital Age

CHAPTER 8

Dynamic Pricing and E-Commerce

Pricing in the Age of Information Technology (IT)

Dynamic pricing is a new name for an old practice. At its heart, dynamic pricing is price discrimination in the world of IT. The fixed-price system that we are most familiar with is actually a relatively recent phenomenon. Before the Industrial Revolution led to assembly lines and large inventories, first-degree price discrimination was the rule rather than the exception. Merchants, rather than large corporations, offered goods and services. Price tags were never affixed to goods and it was up to merchants to extract consumer surplus through haggling.

The seeds of the fixed-price system sprouted when John Wanamaker opened his "Oak Hall" clothing store in Philadelphia in 1861 and promoted his revolutionary "One price and goods returnable" concept. The emergence of factories, assembly lines, and inventories caused fixed prices to become the norm.

In both the haggling and single price world, buyers and sellers sought a mutually acceptable deal. The seller knew that the buyer could take his business elsewhere and the buyer knew that if he didn't make a good enough offer, the seller could sell to another customer. But price comparisons entail "shoe leather." Buyers had to go from store to store to gauge the prices charged by other merchants. And the merchants had to hoof it from place to place to assure their prices were competitive.

Economists usually describe "perfect competition" as a market structure in which many buyers and sellers have perfect information about the prices charged by each firm for an identical good. Absent the geographical constraints of door-to-door price comparisons, perfect competition describes a world in which the forces of supply and demand establish a single price that all buyers and sellers must accept. If a seller attempted to charge any price about the market price, it would lose all of its customers to lower priced competitors.

Although perfect competition is used simply as a model to describe a highly competitive, albeit hypothetical marketplace, the growth of the Internet seemed to give promise that the "law of one price" could indeed prevail. Consumers could compare prices instantaneously with sales shifting to the low-bidder. In such a cut-throat atmosphere, prices were certain to converge to a single figure.

The Internet did not cause the "law of one price" to evolve as predicted. Rather, the World Wide Web became the perfect dispatcher of gains from trade in which innumerable buyers and sellers could, online, find a mutually acceptable price. The price could vary by day, by hour, by minute, and even by customer. "Real-time" got "real fast."

Dynamic pricing is not limited to e-commerce. IT allows brick-and-mortar stores to gauge consumer preferences and their willingness to pay faster than ever before. Beyond increasing revenue and profits, dynamic pricing allows firms to reallocate demand to manage scarce supply constraints. Dynamic pricing is especially useful for goods and services that are perishable. Once a plane leaves the runway, the empty seats cannot be filled. However, perishability is not limited to airlines and hotel rooms. Clothing is seasonal in nature and "perishes" once demand is exhausted. The same can be said for consumer electronics, which become obsolete as new models become available.

There are two categories of dynamic pricing. Posted prices are, as the name implies, prices that customers observe. Price discovery refers to auction mechanisms that allow consumers to determine their own prices.

Posted Prices

Posted prices, whether for e-commerce or traditional stores, can be enhanced by IT, which allows retailers to make pricing and inventory decisions for thousands of products. Consider clothing, which often has a seasonal demand. In the pre-IT days, a line of clothing might have posted fixed prices for up to three months. End-of-season fire sales inevitably followed, with substantial discounts. But with today's technology, brick-and-mortar prices can be raised or lowered on nearly a daily basis, and online prices can change several times/day. When inventory tracking systems show demand for a given line is increasing, prices rise. When a line is moving slowly, prices decrease. In doing so, the firm can use variable pricing to manage its scarce inventory space.

E-commerce provides even more promise for dynamic posted prices. In the pre-Internet days, it was prohibitively costly for firms to attempt to gather customer-specific information and to monitor their buying habits. Mail-order catalogs used zip codes to adjust their prices based on inferred willingness to pay in wealthier regions, but even in those cases, price changes implied creating new catalogs. For retail outlets, price changes meant costly re-tagging.

Today, computer "cookies" allow websites to record the user's previous interactions with the website. "Click-stream" technology allows firms to view user's paths as they browse advertisements, different web pages on the site, and links to other sites. Thus, the retailer not only knows where its customers live, but their history of past purchases, and what goods they've loaded (and unloaded) from online shopping carts. Some online retailers, such as Amazon, may require potential buyers to load goods into the shopping cart just to see their price. Personalized recommendations can be offered to prospective customers based on their past viewing or shopping habits.[1] Unlike costly re-tagging, online prices can be changed by the click of a mouse. This allows for a much more efficient and fast means to segment customers by their willingness to pay.

Determining the optimal markup for online pricing follows the same premise of marginal cost pricing, but with a different twist for the online venue. In addition to wholesale prices, incremental costs include click-through fees on price comparison sites that can range from $0.40 to $1.50. Moreover, conversion rates (the probability that a click will lead to a sale) average only 3%, meaning that a great many clickthrough costs will be incurred for each sale.[2] To illustrate, suppose an online product can be purchased from the wholesaler for $25. Suppose a price comparison site charges $0.50 per click with a conversion rate of 4%. This implies that roughly 25 clicks are necessary to generate a sale (1/.04). Correspondingly, then, the marginal cost of the product is $25 + $0.50 × 25 = $37.50.

The optimal markup depends on the price elasticity of the customers. Earlier in the text, we discussed the potential problems associated with trying to measure price elasticity. Specifically, the calculation assumes the two price/quantity combinations lie on the same demand curve. If they lie on two different demand curves, the coefficient estimate will be biased and could lead to disastrous implications. In the world of traditional pricing, this problem is particularly likely, as firms rarely change their prices unless an outside factor (i.e. one that shifts a demand curve) prompts them to do so. Now, with the ability to change prices rapidly, firms can easily experiment with various prices and gauge the response of consumers. In doing so, the estimated elasticity coefficient will be more realistic.

Beyond varying prices to measure elasticity, online retailers should also change prices to keep their competitors on their toes. The Internet not only allows buyers the chance to comparison shop, it allows firms to monitor the prices of their rival firms. If a firm's price is too stable and predictable, rivals can undercut their prices slightly to allow them to show up as the lowest-priced firm on price comparison sites. A better strategy might be the randomized pricing strategy of undercutting a competitor one day while returning to the original price the next.

Firms with an online presence must realize that online consumers are product-oriented rather than firm-oriented. WalMart may compete with K-Mart in the mass merchandise industry, but online consumers who are looking for a new television are likely to type "televisions" into their search engines rather than type in "WalMart" and seek out its televisions. If a firm only concentrates on its traditional rivals rather than its product-specific competitors, it may find itself consistently undercut in price.

Online retailers should be aware, however, that consumers are wise to such schemes and do not always take kindly to them. In 2000, Amazon.com customers were not pleased to learn that some of them were paying different prices for the same DVDs. One customer deleted the cookies that identified him as a frequent Amazon shopper and he saw the price of a DVD fall from $26.24 to $22.74. Amazon responded that it was part of a "price test" rather than dynamic pricing and offered a refund to customers who paid higher prices. A survey implemented by the Annenberg Public Policy Center of the University of Pennsylvania in 2005 revealed that 76% of respondents stated it would bother them if others paid less than they did for the same products.[3] Eighty-seven percent disagreed with the statement "It's OK if an online store I use charges people different prices for the same products during the same hour." Even more revealing is that 72% disagreed with the following statement: "If a store I shop at frequently charges me lower prices than it charges other people because it wants to keep me as a customer more than it wants to keep them, that's OK." In fact, 64% did not know that it was legal for an online firm to charge different prices to different customers during the same time of day. Seventy-one percent did not know that it was legal for an offline firm to do the same.

Price Discovery

An alternative to posted prices, made possible via e-commerce, is *price discovery*. Price discovery is when the consumer takes an active part in determining the price. A plethora of online retailers such as eBay make products available by auction.

English Auction

The *English auction* is the type of auction most people are familiar with. A single good is made available for sale at an opening bid. Once the bidding stops, the high bidder purchases the good at a price equal to the amount of the bid. Some auction sites allow bidders to submit a price that represents their maximum bid. If a given bidder is outbid, his bid rises automatically. If the latest bid exceeds his reservation price, the bidder drops out of the auction.

Dutch Auction

The *Dutch auction* is essentially the English auction in reverse. The seller initially offers the good at a higher price than buyers are likely to be willing to pay. He gradually lowers the price until he finds a buyer. The Dutch auction was utilized by Google in its initial public offering. The search engine giant initially offered nearly 20 million shares at a price between $108 and $135 per share and gradually lowered it until it eventually reached a price of $85. The Dutch auction raised $1.67 billion for Google.[4]

First-Price, Sealed Bid Auction

A variation on the English auction is the *first-price, sealed bid auction*. Here, the bidders submit a bid without knowing those made by other bidders. The auctioneer gathers up the bids and awards the purchase to the highest bidder. The distinction between the first-price, sealed bid auction and the English auction is that, with the sealed bid auction, the bidders cannot follow the progress of the bids because they are unknown. In addition, whereas the bidder in the English auction can update his bid during the auction, the bidder submits only one bid in the first-price, sealed bid auction.

Second-Price, Sealed Bid Auction

The *second-price, sealed bid auction* (also called the Vickrey auction) bears similarity to the first-price, sealed bid auction to the extent that each bidder submits one sealed bid with the high bidder winning the auction. The difference is that the winning bidder pays a price equal to the second highest bid, rather than his own winning bid. Google uses a second-price, sealed bid auction via AdWords for its online advertising, which annually generates more than $20 billion. Advertisers submit bids in advance based on search terms or keywords. Rather than bid on the price of an impression, advertisers bid on the price they were willing to pay for each click on the advertisement. Sidebar advertisement slots on a results page are sold off in a single auction. Consistent with second-price, sealed bid auctions, the price paid by the winning advertiser is not equal to the winning bid, but rather, is based on the next highest bid.

The AdWords auction is more complex than simply awarding an advertisement to a high bidder. The critical element of online advertising is that the advertisement is tailored to the user's search. To do this, Google tabulates quality scores that determine the relationship between the advertisement and the keyword(s), the quality of the results page to which the advertisement is linked, and the percentage of times users actually click on the advertisement. Advertisement ranks are tabulated by multiplying the advertiser's maximum bid by its quality score. In this manner, advertisers with low quality scores must bid higher to achieve a higher rank. The advertiser with the highest advertisement rank pays the amount bid by the second highest bidder.

To illustrate, suppose two prospective advertisers bid for an advertisement slot. Advertiser A submits a maximum cost per click (CPC) of $2 whereas advertiser B submits a bid of $2.50 CPC. Suppose the quality scores for A and B are 10 and 7, respectively. The corresponding advertisement ranks are $2 x 10, or 20 for advertiser A, and $2.50 x 7, or 15 for advertiser B. Note that even though B is willing to pay a higher CPC, A has the higher advertisement rank. To determine the price A must pay, the second highest advertisement rank (or 15 for B) is divided by A's quality score, resulting in a CPC of 15/10, or $1.50.

The auction is mired in economic theory; in fact, noted Berkeley economist Hal Varian took a leave of absence to become Google's chief economist. The auction was so successfully that Google eventually chucked most of its sales force, which drummed up advertising revenue the old-fashioned way, by wining and dining prospective advertisers, and converted everything onto the online advertisement auction.

The Economics Behind Auctions

Our goal is to determine which auction mechanism generates the most revenue. To understand the incentives underlying auctions, we need to distinguish between **private value auctions** and **common value auctions**. In a private value auction, the bidder wants the good for his personal use, such as bidding for a painting. In a Sotheby's auction of contemporary art, each prospective bidder's reservation price depends not only on the individual's ability to pay, but the satisfaction the bidder derives by owning the work of art. This could vary widely from person to person. In a common value auction, the bidder seeks a good that will generate money for the owner, such as bidding for the rights to an oil field. Hence, the value of the good being auctioned off has approximately the same value to each bidder. If the amount of oil that lies beneath the land were known with certainty, the oil revenue would be largely the same for all bidders. However, because the richness of the land is uncertain, each bidder must estimate the expected revenue from owning the oil rights.

In a private value auction, the bidder knows his reservation price, but does not know the reservation price of the other bidders, which can vary widely according to their tastes. In the English auction, he remains in the bidding until the price rises to a level above his reservation price. At that point, he drops out of the bidding.

To illustrate the various incentives, suppose we have two sports fans, Josh and Jake, who are bidding for an autographed photo of LeBron James. Josh has a reservation price of $200 and Jake has a reservation price of $225. It should be intuitively obvious that in the English auction, the price will rise until Jake bids a price that exceeds $200. In theory, Jake could win with a bid as low as $200.01, providing Jake with consumer surplus equal to $24.99.

We can analyze the English auction strategy from both the bidders' and auctioneer's perspective. From the bidder's point of view, the clear strategy is to remain in the auction until the current bid exceeds one's reservation price. From the auctioneer's perspective, the English auction allows the high bidder to walk away with consumer surplus. The winning bid need not be equal to the winner's true valuation of the good; it need only exceed that of the second-highest bidder.

Let's examine the same scenario, but with a second-price, sealed bid auction. In this case, Josh and Jake cannot observe the progress of the auction. Each bidder must submit exactly one bid. The high bidder wins the auction, but pays a price equal to the bid submitted by the second-highest bidder. Josh values the photo at $200 and Jake is willing to pay up to $225, but neither bidder knows the other's valuation or bid.

What should each person bid? We can begin by acknowledging that each party understands that it will lose the auction if the opponent submits a higher bid. But given that the winning bidder does not pay his own bid, but the second-highest bid, should he submit a bid that is equal to, less than, or higher than his reservation price?

Figure 8.1 illustrates the decision from Josh's perspective. The figure shows four circumstances in which Josh's bid wins the auction. In the first

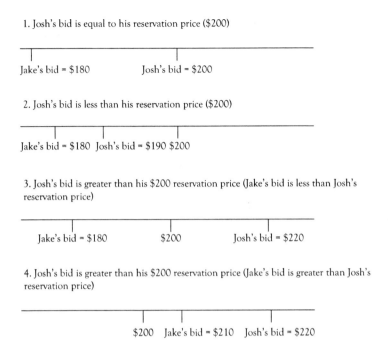

1. Josh's bid is equal to his reservation price ($200)

Jake's bid = $180   Josh's bid = $200

2. Josh's bid is less than his reservation price ($200)

Jake's bid = $180 Josh's bid = $190 $200

3. Josh's bid is greater than his $200 reservation price (Jake's bid is less than Josh's reservation price)

Jake's bid = $180 $200   Josh's bid = $220

4. Josh's bid is greater than his $200 reservation price (Jake's bid is greater than Josh's reservation price)

$200   Jake's bid = $210   Josh's bid = $220

Figure 8.1. Winning bids in a second-price, sealed bid auction.

instance, Josh submits a bid equal to his reservation price ($200). He can only win if Jake submits a bid less than $200. Assuming this is the case then Josh wins the auction, but pays the amount of Jake's bid ($180). Hence, by bidding his valuation, Josh walks away with the photo and $20 in uncaptured consumer surplus.

In the second scenario, Josh submits a winning bid ($190) that is less than his reservation price. As with the first scenario, Josh wins the auction and pays a price equal to Jake's bid ($180), allowing him to have $20 in uncaptured consumer surplus. In comparing the first two scenarios, one should see that it is unambiguously in Josh's interest to submit a bid equal to his reservation price. To win, his bid must exceed Jake's, but the price Josh pays is equal to $180 (Jakes' bid) regardless of his own bid. Because Josh cannot control Jake's bid (and, in fact, does not know Jake's bid), raising his own bid to reflect his valuation of the photo increases his likelihood of winning the auction without affecting the price he pays if he wins.

Scenarios three and four illustrate the possibilities if Josh wins with a bid that exceeds his reservation price. Josh might consider this possibility because he will not have to pay the amount of his bid if he wins. In scenario three, Josh submits a bid of $220 and Jake submits a bid of $180. Because Josh submitted the higher bid, he wins the auction, pays the amount of Jake's bid, and walks away with $20 in uncaptured consumer surplus. Note that the outcome is identical to the case in which Josh submitted a bid equal to his valuation; he still wins the auction, he pays Jake's bid, and he earns $20 in consumer surplus. Thus, it did not benefit Josh to submit the higher bid.

Scenario four indicates the worst case scenario for Josh. He submits a bid of $220 and Jake submits a bid of $210. Josh wins the auction, but must pay a price that exceeds his valuation of the photo. In comparing scenarios three and four, we can see why Josh would never submit a bid that exceeds his reservation price. Either the result is identical to when he bids an amount equal to his reservation price, or he wins the auction, but must pay more than what the photo is worth to him.

Combining all four scenarios, it should be obvious that Josh should submit a bid equal to his reservation price. We could re-create an identical set of circumstances for Jake, but the results will be the same. Not knowing what Josh will bid, Jake is unambiguously better off submitting a bid equal to his own valuation ($225). Jake will win the auction and will pay $200 for the photo (i.e. Josh's bid).

Note that the results of the second-price, sealed bid auction are virtually identical to those of the English auction. In the English auction, the bids rise until Jake submits a price that exceeds Josh's reservation price. In theory, this could be as low as $200.01. With the second-price, sealed bid auction, both parties submit a bid equal to their reservation price, Jake wins the auction and pays $200, which is Josh's valuation of the photo.

Now let's compare the results of the Dutch and first-price, sealed bid auctions. Recall that in the Dutch auction, the price gradually falls until one of the bidders claims the good. In the first-price, sealed bid auction, the bidders submit a single bid without knowing the bids submitted by the other bidders. The high bidder pays a price equal to his bid.

Continuing with Josh and Jake, the Dutch auction begins with a price that exceeds each party's valuation. Because the winning bidder must pay the price at which he bids, it makes no sense for either party to claim the good until the price drops to his reservation price. Thus, Jake will hold off until the price falls to $225. Should he claim the photo and pay $225 or should he hold off in the hope that he can get the photo at a lower price?

This is what distinguishes the Dutch auction from the English or second-price, sealed bid auctions. In the English auction, Jake will gradually up the bid until Josh drops out of the auction. Although Jake does not have information as to Josh's bid in the second-price, sealed bid auction, his incentive is to submit a bid equal to his reservation price, knowing that if he wins, he will pay the second-highest bid and earn consumer surplus.

But the Dutch auction requires a guessing game on Jake's part. He knows that Josh's reservation price does not exceed $225 (otherwise Josh would have won the auction), but does not know with certainty the price that will cause Josh to claim the photo. If Jake claims the photo at $225, he earns no consumer surplus, but if he allows the price to fall, he may still be able to win the auction and pay a lower price. Thus, allowing the price to continue to fall involves a trade-off: on the one hand, it might allow Jake to win the auction at a lower price. On the other hand, by allowing the price to drop, Jake gambles that Josh will claim the photo. If Jake had perfect information, he would know that he could wait until the price fell to $200.01. Absent such knowledge, Jake must weigh the benefits of allowing the price to fall against its costs.

Interestingly, the bidders' incentives in the first-price, sealed bid auction are identical to those of the Dutch auction. As with the Dutch auction, the winner must pay the amount of his bid; hence, it would make no sense for a bidder in the first-price, sealed bid auction to submit a bid that exceeds his reservation price. In addition, the bidder has no knowledge of the other bidders' valuation at the time he submits a bid.

The thought process, therefore, replicates that of the Dutch auction. Because Jake will never submit a bid that exceeds his valuation of the photo ($225), his best chance of winning the auction is to submit a bid equal to $225. However, by submitting a bid that is less than $225, he must balance the decreased odds of winning the auction against the potential benefits of winning the auction at a lower price.

Thus far, we've established that the revenues generated from the English auction should be identical to those generated from the second-price, sealed bid auction, and that the revenue generated from the Dutch auction should be identical to that generated from the first-price, sealed bid auction. But which is likely to generate the most revenue: the English/second-price auction or the Dutch/first-price auction?

Perhaps surprisingly, the revenues generated from any of the four auctions should be the same.[5] This is predicated on several assumptions. First, the bidders are neutral in their attitudes toward risk. Second, whereas the bidders recognize that reservation prices differ across bidders, they assume that all bidders follow the same set of strategies regarding bids. Just as Jake weighs the benefits of allowing the price to fall below $225 against its costs, so does Josh weigh the costs and benefits of allowing the price to fall below $200. Moreover, the optimal set of bids should be such that, after all bids are simultaneously revealed, no individual bidder can be better off by unilaterally changing his bid. Given these assumptions, bidders in the first-price, sealed bid auction will estimate the second highest bid and submit that figure. Bidders in the Dutch auction will claim the good just before the second highest bidder claims it. On average, therefore, all four auction mechanisms should generate the same revenue.

This finding (called the Revenue Equivalence Theorem) should not be inferred as suggesting that the revenues from the four auctions will be identical, but rather, that they will be the same *on average*. Because the English and second-price auctions are based on simple strategies and do not involve the guesswork inherent in the Dutch and first-price, sealed bid strategies, the variation in revenues will be smaller with the English and second-price auctions.

Can the firm increase the revenues generated from the auction? Indeed, this can be accomplished in two ways. First, the greater the number of bidders, the greater the number of reservation prices. Logically, therefore, the greater the number of bidders, the smaller the gap between the winning bid and the second-highest bid. This implication should be fairly intuitive. Our analysis suggests that Jake will win the auction and pay a price that equals (or is just slightly more) than Josh's valuation. As more bidders enter the auction, it would seem rather unlikely that all of them will value the photo less than Josh. If only one of them values the photo more than Josh, the price paid for the photo will rise even if Jake still wins the auction. Moreover, one of the bidders may value the photo more than Jake. If so, another bidder will win the auction and the price will be at least equal to Jake's bid (or higher if other bidders value the photo more than he does).

Another tool is for the seller to include a minimum selling price. If the bids do not exceed this price, the seller does not sell the item. If the bids exceed the minimum price, the good is sold to the highest bidder with the price determined by the auction mechanism. How can this increase the seller's revenue? To begin with, one can easily see that the minimum selling price has no impact if at least two bids exceed the minimum. If the minimum selling price for the LeBron James photo is $150 and Josh and Jake value the photo at $200 and $225, respectively, then the Revenue Equivalence Theorem suggests that Jake will win the auction, pay $200 (or $200.01) for the photo, and earn roughly $25 in consumer surplus. But what if the minimum selling price was set at $210? Jake must bid at least $210 to obtain the photo, even though Josh would never have offered to pay more than $200. Jake still wins the auction, but pays $210 and earns only $15 in consumer surplus. Given that the seller does not know the valuations for either Jake or Josh, the only risk incurred by the seller is setting a minimum price that exceeds either valuation. For example, if the seller had established a minimum price of $230, neither individual would have bid for the photo.

Thus far, we have assumed that the bidders in the private value auction were risk neutral. How would the results differ if they were risk averse? In the case of the English auction, risk attitudes do not matter. The bids rise until all of the bidders except one have dropped out. Because losing bids pay nothing, the winner controls the amount of the winning bid. The same is true for the second-price, sealed bid auction. As noted earlier, each bidder has an incentive to submit his own valuation as the bid. This effectively eliminates the role that risk attitudes may play in the auction.

The incentives for bidders in the first-price, sealed bid and Dutch auctions are, however, influenced by risk attitudes. Recall that no bidder would submit a bid that exceeds his reservation price under any of the auction mechanisms. In both the first-price, sealed bid and Dutch auctions, however, the bidder can maximize his odds of winning the auction at an acceptable price by bidding at his reservation price. This is most obvious with the Dutch auction. As soon as the price falls to his reservation price, he can claim the item. With the first-price, sealed bid auction, the bidder can submit his reservation price as his bid. Although he cannot guarantee that he will win the auction, he maximizes his likelihood of doing so without risking that he pays more for the good than what it is worth to him.

As noted earlier, however, rather than volunteer to pay his reservation price, the bidder can allow the price to fall in the Dutch auction (or submit a price that is less than his reservation price in the first-price, sealed bid auction) in the hope that he can still win the auction, but pay a lower price. By choosing this route, the bidder risks that he will not be outbid; hence, trying to win the auction at a lower price is something of a gamble. Risk-averse bidders will be less willing to take that chance. Hence, one would expect risk-averse bidders to submit a price that is closer to their reservation price in the first-price, sealed bid auction (or alternatively, not allow the price to drop as much in the Dutch auction). This implies that the average revenue in the Dutch/first-price, sealed bid auction will be greater with risk-averse bidders than with risk neutral bidders.

In summary, when the bidders are risk neutral, all four auction mechanisms are expected, on average, to generate the same revenue. If the bidders are risk averse, the first-price, sealed bid and Dutch auctions will generate more revenue than the second price, sealed bid or English auctions. What does this suggest for the firm? The implications are that in a private value auction, the firm should use either the first-price, sealed bid or Dutch auction. Assuming the seller does not know the risk preferences of the bidder, the first-price, sealed bid or Dutch will generate the same revenue as the other auction mechanisms if the bidders are risk neutral, but would generate more revenue if the bidders are risk averse.

In a common value auction, the value of the good is roughly the same across bidders, but is not known to any bidder with certainty. Imagine, for example, bidding for a jar of pennies. All bidders see the jar, but none of them know with certainty how many pennies are in the jar; they can only estimate the number. Clearly, in such a scenario, some people will overestimate the number of pennies whereas others will underestimate it. Consequently, if the jar was auctioned off to the high bidder, the winner will be the person who overestimates the number of pennies by the largest margin! Economists refer to this situation as the **winner's curse**.

One can sense the uneasiness that must come with winning a common value auction. After all, given that the true value of the good must be more or less the same across all bidders, the winner realizes that all of the opposing bidders thought the good was worth less than he did.

Theory suggests that bidders will incorporate the likelihood of the winner's curse into their bidding strategies and bid more cautiously as a result. The bidder begins by assuming that if he wins the auction, his estimate of the value of the good is probably too high. In essence, he presumes that he would be afflicted with the winner's curse if he submitted a bid equal to his unbiased valuation of the good. Assuming that the competing bidders think the same way, he submits a bid equal to what he believes is the second-highest valuation.

Winning the common value auction without overbidding is no easy task. It requires the bidder to not only estimate the value of the good, but also the expected error from overbidding. Hence, the bid should be equal to the bidder's estimate of the true value of the good less the expected error of the winning bidder. The more precise the estimate is, the lower the amount by which one must reduce one's bid. Using a sports analogy, it is a lot easier to a club to bid for a marginal-free agent than for a star-free agent. In addition to fluctuating performances, professional athletes subject themselves to potential injuries. A star player on the disabled list has no more value to his team than a marginal player on the bench, and may even be worth less. Overestimation errors for marginal players will tend to be smaller than those made with star players. Thus, it's easier to estimate the value of a player with a relatively short career than it is to estimate the value of a star player whose career may span two decades or two months.

One important distinction between the private value and common value auction is that, whereas the value one places on owning a specific good can vary greatly across individuals, the value of the good in the common value auction should not vary between bidders. This is important because the bids in a common value auction can signal important information to other bidders about the true value of the good.

This can be most easily illustrated in the English auction. A bidder may have formulated a notion of the good's common value before the auction begins. But if the bids increase at a snail's pace, and remain well below the bidder's initial assessment of the product's worth, the individual may begin to question his reservation price and adjust downward. At the opposite extreme, if the bids rapidly pass one's own reservation price, the individual may infer that he underestimated the value of the good and should increase his bid. Because each bid conveys useful information as to the estimated values from opposing bidders, the winner's curse is likely to be less extreme.

In a Dutch auction, the bidders receive no information to help them gauge whether they are overbidding. The same holds true for the first-price, sealed bid auction. They submit a single bid with no ex ante knowledge of the value estimates placed on the good by the other bidders. In both cases, they must pay a price equal to their bid. Although one might infer that the Dutch and first-price, sealed bid auctions will be more lucrative than an English auction, the reverse is true. Bidders tend to be well aware of the potential for the winner's curse and the lack of opportunities to reassess their estimates in the Dutch/first-price, sealed bid auctions. To avoid the possibility of the winner's curse, they tend to be more cautious in their bidding than they would have been with the English auction.

From the bidder's perspective, the second-price, sealed bid auction is modestly better. Although the bidder infers no information as to the estimated values submitted by the other bidders, the price is determined in part by the estimates of the other bidders. This entices him to be less cautious when submitting a bid.

Putting the pieces together, the feature that distinguishes the private value auction from the common value auction is that, in the latter, the good should have roughly the same value to all bidders. Thus, the bids convey useful information as to the true value of the good. Absent this information, bidders tend to bid more cautiously to avoid the winner's curse. Although the bidders are not privy to the others' bids in the second-price, sealed bid auction, the fact that the price will be equal to the second-highest bid causes them to be less cautious. Hence, from the seller's perspective, the English auction tends to generate the most revenue, followed by the second-price, sealed bid auction, and then the Dutch/first-price, sealed bid auction. This rank order remains the same even if the bidders are risk averse.

Summary

- Dynamic pricing has become possible through advances in IT. It allows firms to adjust their prices much more quickly to speed the sale of slow-moving merchandise or otherwise adjust prices to reflect inventories and inventory costs.
- IT allows firms to gather consumer-specific information that allows them to price to each consumer individually online.
- Pricing for e-commerce should include not only wholesale prices, but also click-through fees and conversion rates.
- E-commerce offers a better opportunity for firms to gauge the level of price sensitivity as prices can be altered on a daily basis (or even more frequently).
- Firms listing products for e-commerce should be careful not to make their prices too easy for competitors to monitor. If prices can be monitored too easily, competitors can under-price them by only a few cents and have their product pop up as less expensive on search bots.
- Unlike traditional retail outlets, e-commerce competitors may be product-specific rather than store-specific.
- Price discovery exists when the prospective customer actively assumes a role in determining the price, usually through online auctions.
- In an English auction, the customer who bids the highest gets to purchase the good, with the price equal to his bid.
- In a Dutch auction, the seller puts the product out for auction at a price that exceeds what buyers are willing to pay, and then gradually lowers the price until he finds a buyer.
- In a first-price, sealed bid auction, each bidder submits a sealed bid with no knowledge of the bids submitted by others. The high bidder purchases the good at a price equal to his bid. In a second-price, sealed bid auction, each bidder submits a sealed bid with no knowledge of the bids submitted by others. The high bidder purchases the good at a price equal to the bid of the second-highest bidder.

- In a private value auction, all four auction mechanisms should generate the same expected revenue if the bidders are risk neutral. Sellers can generate more revenue by increasing the number of bidders or by establishing a minimum price for the good. If the bidders are risk-averse, the first-price, sealed bid and Dutch auctions should generate the most revenue, followed by the second-price, sealed bid and English auctions.

- In a common value auction, the good should have roughly the same value to all bidders. Hence, the winning bid often goes to the bidder who overestimated the true value of the good by the greatest amount (winner's curse). Bidders are aware of the winner's curse and strategically attempt to incorporate it into their bids.

- In a common value auction, the English auction should generate the most revenue, followed by the second-price sealed bid auction. The first-price, sealed bid auction should generate the same revenue as the reverse and Dutch auctions. The rank order is the same regardless of the risk preferences of the bidders.

CHAPTER 9

Legal and Ethical Issues

Legal Issues Surrounding Price Discrimination

We would be remiss if we did not discuss the legal issues surrounding price discrimination. At face value, the **Robinson–Patman Act of 1936** appears to declare price discrimination illegal. However, the language in Sec. 2(a) bars price discrimination only if its intent is anticompetitive in nature:

> It shall be unlawful for any person engaged in commerce, in the course of such commerce, either directly or indirectly, to discriminate in price between different purchasers of commodities of like grade and quality, where either or any of the purchases involved in such discrimination are in commerce, where such commodities are sold for use, consumption, or resale within the United States or any Territory thereof or the District of Columbia or any insular possession or other place under the jurisdiction of the United States, and where the effect of such discrimination may be substantially to lessen competition or tend to create a monopoly in any line of commerce, or to injure, destroy, or prevent competition with any person who either grants or knowingly receives the benefit of such discrimination, or with customers of either of them.

In judging whether a firm has violated the Robinson–Patman Act, the courts have focused on "***primary line injury***" and "***secondary line injury***." Primary line injury occurs when the firm offering the discount threatens competition between itself and competing sellers. An example would be a firm that prices its good below its average variable cost for a significant period of time to drive rival firms out of business.

The case of *Utah Pie* versus *Continental Baking* offers insights into primary line injury. Utah Pie, a family-owned business, entered the frozen pie industry in Salt Lake City in the 1950s and quickly established market share, selling pies at a price of $4.15/dozen. Four years later, when price competition with its three largest competitors, Continental Baking, Carnation, and Pet, caused its price to fall to $2.75/dozen, the firm filed suit. The courts ruled for the plaintiff largely on the basis that the prices charged in Salt Lake City were significantly lower than what was being charged in other geographic markets. In fact, Pet did not deny that it suffered losses in the Salt Lake City market.

Secondary line injury occurs when the discriminatory act harms the competition between the favored customer who receives the discounted price and the disfavored rival firms. An example of secondary line injury is the case of *FTC* versus *Morton Salt*. Morton Salt offered quantity discounts on it premium Blue Label salt. Although the discounts were purportedly available to all supermarkets, only the largest customers, such as A&P, were capable of buying sufficiently large quantities to qualify for the discount. This would allow the large national chains to set retail prices that undercut the smaller Mom & Pop supermarkets. The intent of the Robinson–Patman Act, as expressed by Justice Black in the FTC versus Morton Salt case, is to assure that price discrimination is not implemented to reduce the level of competition:

> "[I]n enacting the Robinson–Patman Act, Congress was especially concerned with protecting small businesses which were unable to buy in quantities, such as the merchants here who purchased in less-than-carload lots."

Not all acts of price discrimination violate the Robinson–Patman Act. Sec. 2(a) establishes that cost-related or quantity-related discounts are acceptable under the law:

> That nothing herein contained shall prevent differentials which make only due allowance for differences in the cost of manufacture, sale, or delivery resulting from the differing methods or quantities in which such commodities are to such purchasers sold or delivered.

The final component of Sec. 2(a) allows for most market-driven forms of price discrimination to take place legally:

> That nothing herein contained shall prevent persons engaged in selling goods, wares, or merchandise in commerce from selecting their own customers in bona fide transactions and not in restraint of trade: And provided further, That nothing herein contained shall prevent price changes from time to time where in response to changing conditions affecting the market for or the marketability of the goods concerned, such as but not limited to actual or imminent deterioration of perishable goods, obsolescence of seasonal goods, distress sales under court process, or sales in good faith in discontinuance of business in the goods concerned.

The Supreme Court has also allowed for ***functional discounts***. A functional discount exists when the purchaser is part of the supplier's distribution system. The implied assumption is that the discount is a reimbursement for the purchaser's distribution or marketing functions.

Ironically, the Robinson–Patman Act is much maligned by both economists and antitrust scholars. Economic theory suggests that price discrimination allows firms to profitably reach market segments they would otherwise ignore. Other critics assert that the intent of the Act should be to prohibit anticompetitive behavior rather than to protect the financial interests of rivals. In a scholarly article printed in the *Journal of Law and Economics*, Thomas Ross offered this searing indictment of the Robinson–Patman Act:

> The Robinson–Patman Act has the distinction of being almost universally unpopular among antitrust scholars. This is probably because it looks less like an antitrust measure than like legislative relief for small business. That the law wears an antitrust cloak is probably a measure of the cunning of its original proponents.

When the innumerable exceptions to the Robinson–Patman Act are considered, most practices described in this textbook would fall within the range of acceptability. Note that the language emphasizes the effects on competition and that most cases brought before the court involve wholesalers and retailers rather than final users.

Ethical Issues Surrounding Price Discrimination

The economic perspective of price discrimination is largely positive. If the Robinson–Patman Act were strictly enforced, price-sensitive consumers would frequently be denied various goods and services. If an airline was required to charge the same fare for all of its clientele, it would cater to the less price-sensitive business customer. As the tables in this textbook have repeatedly shown, it would be more profitable to charge the business-class price and allow seats to remain empty than to lower the price for all customers to assure no seat goes unoccupied. Given the high fixed costs of operating an airline, one wonders if the airline could even generate profits absent the ability to price discriminate. At the very least, fewer flights would be available. In fact, the airline industry has a long history of financial struggles even with price discrimination. If the Robinson–Patman Act was strictly enforced, the number of available flights would decrease and more airlines would cease operations entirely.

The view that price discrimination is beneficial to consumers does not appear to be shared by the prospective customers. Intertemporal price discrimination (a.k.a. price skimming) is quite commonplace, particularly with electronics, yet the $200 iPhone price cut was not well received. Various forms of second-degree price discrimination, such as coupons, have existed for years. But when Netflix introduced Qwikster as a way to get its customers to self-select between DVDs and the less expensive downloads, it was met with so much resistance that it eliminated Qwikster and reverted to its traditional service. Third-degree price discrimination is not new to the business world. Discounts for children and senior citizens have been established practices for decades. Hard-copy, mail-order catalogs routinely listed different prices based on the zip codes of the recipients. Yet Amazon drew a lot of flak for selling the same DVDs to different customers for different prices based on their inferred willingness to pay. Why is "traditional" price discrimination accepted whereas dynamic pricing on the Internet is met with such resistance?

Research by Nobel Prize winning economist Daniel Kahneman on fairness may provide some insights.[1] Kahneman noted various determinants of fairness judgments. A **reference transaction** refers to a price/profit precedent on which buyers and sellers rely. The assumption is that the reference price allows the firm to earn a fair profit. Hence, any effort to increase its profit by raising the price is perceived to be unfair. At the same time, buyers believe that firms are entitled to their reference profit. Hence, if conditions cause the firms' profits to decrease, the firms may increase their prices to restore their profits. Buyers infer such behavior as fair.

This suggests that price increases to capture one's willingness to pay are deemed to be unfair whereas raising prices to accommodate increases in the cost of production is justified. However, even if costs do not increase, Kahneman found that price increases are justified if other firms raise their prices. In essence, the fact that other firms are increasing prices suggests a change in the reference price. Interestingly, the key factor is that the behavior is perceived as normal rather than just.

Another determinant of fairness is how the outcomes are "coded" by consumers. Price changes that increase one's wealth at the expense of another tend to be viewed as unfair. Out-of-pocket costs trump opportunity costs, and actual losses are perceived as more important than foregone profits. This differs from the viewpoint of economists, who tend to view them as identical. Thus, a price increase that raises the firm's profits is more likely to be viewed as unfair than one that is implemented to avoid a loss.

Along these lines, respondents in the Kahneman et al. study were given two hypothetical scenarios, and were asked to comment as to whether the firm's behavior was fair or unfair. In the first, an auto dealer, accustomed to selling at list price, reacted to a shortage by raising his price by $200. The respondents viewed his behavior as unfair. In the second setting, an auto dealer who customarily offered buyers a $200 discount from the list price, decided to start charging customers the list price. Although the consumers were going to pay $200 more for cars in this scenario as well, the respondents regarded the dealer's actions to be fair, but by a relatively small margin. Because the list price serves as a reference price, the respondents coded the first scenario as an unambiguous gain to the firm. In the second setting, the response depended on whether the respondent coded the discounted price or the list price as the reference price.

Kahneman's research has some interesting implications for J.C. Penney's bold new pricing strategy. Rather than having a barrage of sales indicating marked-down prices, the discounted prices will become the standard prices. No longer will items sport a tag showing the nondiscounted and discounted prices side by side. Unlike WalMart, the intent is not to make J.C. Penney the low-priced leader, but merely to establish more predictable pricing.

But many behavioral economists are not so sure that J.C. Penney's "permanently discounted prices" will go over well. To many consumers, the "standard price" represents the reference price. Hence, any marked-down price is a bargain. Without the undiscounted price serving as a reference, the "permanently discounted price" may be viewed as the reference price, causing the consumers to infer no bargain.

The psychology of reference pricing may explain why various forms of price discrimination were not regarded to be controversial. In the context of children's and senior citizen discounts, the price paid by the other patrons was regarded as the reference price. The discounts received by children and seniors were perceived as gains to specific consumers. One would expect the reaction to be different if the discounted prices were marketed as the "normal" price, with "surcharges" to all other buyers. The same undoubtedly rings true for coupons. The undiscounted price is perceived to be the reference price. The coupons represent a gain to coupon-holders.

Along these lines, one assumes that the reaction to Qwikster took Netflix by surprise. As the less-expensive download option for rentals was increasing in popularity, Netflix sought to pass the savings onto its customers in terms of lower prices for online-only services. The assumption was that its customer base would self-select based on preferences. Those with quality downloading capabilities would choose the cheaper service, whereas those who did not would opt for the traditional mail-order DVD rentals. But because traditional customers subscribed to Netflix primarily for mail-order DVD rentals, and were given the ability to download movies for the same monthly charge as that sector of the market began to develop, splitting the services was inferred as doubling the price of the existing subscription. Thus, the reference price was entrenched in the minds of consumers such that the saw themselves as being overcharged, rather than being offered a less expensive option for renting movies.

Kahneman et al.'s research defines price changes that are likely to be perceived as fair. Respondents seem to believe that firms are entitled to their reference profit. Consequently, increases in wholesale or operating costs may be met with price hikes without causing consumers to feel betrayed. This does not imply that consumers expect firms to lower their prices to keep their profits constant. When asked how a firm should respond to a decrease in the cost of production, half thought it was acceptable for the firm to keep its price constant and pocket the additional profit. Less than a third thought the price should drop by the amount of the decrease in unit cost.

The public also believes firms act unfairly when they raise prices in response to excess demand. One of the most basic tenets of supply and demand is that, when confronted with a shortage, firms raise prices to clear the market. In doing so, production will increase and more transactions will occur at the higher price than would have occurred had the price remained constant. This perspective is not shared by respondents to Kahneman's survey. Thus, whereas it is acceptable for a firm to increase its price to response to an increase in costs (a.k.a. a decrease in market supply), it is unethical for a firm to raise its price in response to an increase in market demand.

Further, when given a scenario in which a store had but one unit remaining on its shelf, the respondents thought it would be unfair for the store to auction off the last unit. Ironically, when the question added a phrase suggesting that a portion of the proceeds would go toward a charity, the percentage of respondents who judged the behavior to be unfair dropped dramatically. Putting the two scenarios together, individuals appear to be more averse to the perception that the firm gained in the transaction than to the reality that they might have to pay a higher price.

Economic research on fairness also shows that consumers will punish firms that are perceived to behave unfairly even if it goes against their own self-interest. A great deal of research has been performed on the "ultimatum game." One subject is given a sum of money and is permitted to offer any percentage of it to another subject. If the subject accepts the offer, the money is split in accordance with the offer. If the offer is refused, neither subject gets any money. In theory, the self-interest of the subject making the offer is maximized by making the lowest possible nonzero offer. For example, if the subject is given $100 to split with the other subject, and he offers her $1, she would rather accept the dollar than to refuse it and gain nothing. This is rarely what the experimental findings show. Most offers are at or near 50%. Perhaps more surprising is the finding that sometimes the offers are refused. These subjects would rather punish the unfair offer even if it causes them to be worse off as well. Extrapolating these results to the real world, fear of punishment may cause profit-maximizing firms not to act in their own short-term interests if it implies losing goodwill (and future profits).

What does all of this suggest for e-tailers? The actions taken by Apple with the iPhone, Amazon, and Netflix reflect textbook examples of how innovative pricing strategies can be used to capture consumer surplus and increase profits. And despite the fact that price discrimination is hardly a new concept, the pricing strategies adopted by Apple, Amazon, and Netflix were greeted with controversy and disdain. In the context of Kahneman's research, firms need to be cognizant of when price discriminatory acts will be viewed as acceptable or exploitative. As research on the ultimatum game demonstrates, consumers are willing to punish firms that behave unfairly to their own detriment.

Nonetheless, Kahneman also noted that psychological studies of adaptation show that any stable state of affairs is eventually accepted. Perhaps the fallout regarding the iPhone, Amazon DVDs, and Netflix subscription prices merely reflected the fact that e-commerce is still evolving. As stated earlier, haggling over prices dominated markets until the Industrial Revolution. Consumers had to adapt to the concept of fixed, posted prices, and eventually they did. Perhaps the e-world, with its movements toward personalized prices and transactions, will become the new norm, and eventually be embraced by consumers.

Summary

- The Robinson–Patman Act makes it illegal to charge different prices for the same good if the effect is to lessen competition.
- Although the general intent of price discrimination is to allow the firm to profitably reach the more price sensitive market segment, consumers may react angrily if they realize prices differ across individuals.

Table of Strategies

Comparison of Price-Discrimination Strategies

Strategy	Description	Benefits	Risk/Costs	Necessary conditions
First-degree price discrimination (Chapter 5)	Each unit is sold for the maximum price each buyer is willing to pay	1. No alternative strategy is more profitable 2. Allows the firm to price the more price sensitive buyer into the market	1. Buyers have an incentive to disguise their willingness to pay 2. Ability to extract full willingness to pay is unlikely	1. Must have some degree of market power 2. Must be able to prevent resale of the good 3. Knowledge of each buyer's willingness to pay
Quantity discounts (Chapter 6)	The buyer is offered a quantity at an average price that is lower than the sum of the prices of each unit	Can entice the buyer to purchase more units than he would if priced individually	Buyer might resell the discounted unit at a higher price	1. Must have some degree of market power 2. Must be able to prevent resale of the good
Quality choices (Chapter 6)	The firm offers two versions of the same product that differ in quality	Allows buyers with greater willingness to pay to purchase the premium good without sacrificing revenues from others	Consumers may not place sufficient value on the premium good to justify the price increase necessary to cover costs	Differences in costs must be small in comparison to differences in prices
Bundling (Chapter 6)	The consumer is offered two or more products for one price rather than selling each good individually	Some buyers who would not have purchased all of the goods may buy the bundle	Some consumers who would have purchased one of the goods may not be willing to purchase the bundle	Relative valuations of the goods must differ across consumers

(Continued)

Comparison of Price-Discrimination Strategies—(Continued)

Strategy	Description	Benefits	Risk/Costs	Necessary conditions
Mixed Bundling (Chapter 6)	Allowing consumers to choose either the bundle or the individually priced goods	May entice consumers who value at least one good below unit cost to buy the bundle	Can lose revenue from customers who would have been willing to buy the individually priced goods	1. Relative valuations of the goods must differ across consumers. 2. Some consumers value at least one of the goods less than its unit cost
Tying (Chapter 6)	Pricing one good relatively low to increase sales of a complementary good	1. Lost profit contribution is more than made up with higher profit contribution on complementary good 2. Allows firms to meter demand	Could lose consumers if switching costs are low	1. Switching costs must be relatively high 2. Some tying may be illegal
Two-part tariff (Chapter 6)	Charging an entry fee and a separate unit price	The entry fee captures some consumer surplus without decreasing unit sales	If the entry fee is too high, will lose the more price sensitive buyer	The higher the unit price, the lower the entry fee
Price skimming (Chapter 6)	Charging a high introductory price and then lowering it later on	1. Captures some consumer surplus of buyers who want to be the first to own the good 2. Later, the firm prices to attract the more price sensitive buyers	1. The high introductory price encourages market entry 2. High unit costs at low volume may cancel out higher prices 3. Could anger buyers if the price drops too quickly after introduction	1. Unit costs of small volume is not prohibitively high 2. A sufficient number of buyers are willing to pay a premium to obtain the good

Strategy	Description	Result	Problems	Conditions
Penetration (Chapter 6)	Pricing the good below unit cost to attract buyers and then raising the price after brand loyalty is established	1. Reduction in profit contribution at the front end is more than made up with higher profit contribution as prices rise 2. Low introductory price deters market entry	1. May attract price sensitive buyers who switch brands after prices rise 2. The firm may not be able to meet demand at the low introductory price	1. Product must be re-purchased frequently 2. Best when economies of scale exist in production 3. Works best when product demand is relatively elastic
Peak-load pricing (Chapter 6)	Setting higher prices during periods of peak demand	Re-distributes demand during peak periods	1. Metering costs may be high 2. High prices may be viewed as unfair by consumers who are unable to switch out of peak periods	1. Marginal cost of meeting demand during peak periods is high 2. The good cannot be stored
Third-degree price discrimination (Chapter 7)	Separating buyers into groups based on price sensitivity and setting separate prices for each group	More profitable than charging a single price for everyone	1. Consumers may purchase lower priced good and resell it to less price sensitive buyers 2. Loss of goodwill if consumers resent differential pricing	1. Must be able to readily identify group membership 2. Must be able to prevent re-sale 3. Competing firms cannot charge a lower price to attract the less price sensitive buyers

Comparison of Auction Types

Types of auctions	Description	Private-value auction profitability, risk-neutral bidders	Private-value auction profitability, risk-averse bidders	Common-value auction profitability
English auction (Chapter 8)	Consumers bid until all other drop out of bidding	Same profitability as other auction types	No effect on bids, same profitability as second-price, sealed bid auction	Most profitable because bidders are less weary of the winner's curse
First-price, sealed bid auction (Chapter 8)	Bidders submit sealed bids. High bidder pays a price equal to his bid	Same profitability as other auction types	Most profitable, same as Dutch auction because bidders bid closer to their reservation price	Least profitable, same as Dutch auction because bidders are most concerned with the winner's curse
Second-price, sealed bid auction (Chapter 8)	Bidders submit sealed bids. High bidder pays a price equal to second highest bid	Same profitability as other auction types	No effect on bids, same profitability as English auction	Less profitable than English auction, but more profitable than first-price, sealed bid or Dutch auction
Dutch auction (Chapter 8)	Sellers sets initially high price and gradually lowers it until a buyer is found	Same profitability as other auction types	Most profitable, same as first-price, sealed-bid auction because bidders bid closer to their reservation price	Least profitable, same as first-price, sealed bid auction because bidders are most concerned with the winner's curse

Notes

Chapter 1

1. Gregorowicz and Hegji (1998).
2. For a more thorough critique of the managerial economics curriculum, see Marburger (2011).

Chapter 2

1. Oswald (2011).
2. U.S. Food and Drug Administration (2009).

Chapter 3

1. Energy Information Administration (2011).
2. Dietz (2008).
3. Welsh (2011).
4. Economists often use regression analysis to statistically estimate a demand curve. When estimated accurately, it allows for a more precise measurement of the elasticity coefficient.

Chapter 4

1. For simplicity's sake, this analysis admittedly omits the opportunity cost of Wendy's time. If the price is not high enough, she may opt for leisure time.

Chapter 5

1. Converting the example to reflect manufacturing is straightforward. Instead of making production decisions one unit at a time, they would be made one batch at a time. In either case, these decisions can be made by comparing marginal revenue and marginal cost.
2. http://www.rolltide.com/boosters/alab-boosters.html
3. Stecklow (1996).
4. Stecklow (1996).

5. Wald (1998).
6. Netessine and Shumsky (2002).
7. Netessine and Shumsky (2002).

Chapter 6

1. There may be some overlap in distinguishing between the price discrimination strategies. The Disney example used earlier would have constituted bundling if the three-day package allowed the buyer to visit three specific theme parks (i.e. the Magic Kingdom, EPCOT, and Animal Kingdom), as opposed to three park visits (which would allow the patron to visit the Magic Kingdom on three separate days).
2. Had the revenue-maximizing price for the bundle been less than $95, the revenue collected by the firm would actually be lower than if the services were priced separately.
3. Technically, the firm would offer the bundle for $174.99. Otherwise, Byron would be indifferent between the bundle and buying the three products individually.
4. Evers (2006).
5. Based on figures from online booking at www.loewshotels.com.
6. Litman (2011).

Chapter 8

1. I must admit, however, that Facebook was off the mark when they offered me links to The Scooter Store and Dentu-Crème. The last straw was when it offered up an ad for NHL apparel, asking me (an avid Pittsburgh Penguins fan) whether I thought Penguins star Sidney Crosby or archrival Capitals center Alex Ovechkin should win the scoring title.
2. Baye et al. (2007).
3. Annenberg Public Policy Center (2005).
4. Elgin (2004).
5. Vickrey (1961).

Chapter 9

1. Kahneman, Knetsch, and Thaler (1986).

References

Annenberg Public Policy Center at the University of Pennsylvania. (2005). *Annenberg Study shows Americans vulnerable to exploitation in the online and offline marketplace.* Retrieved January 4, 2012, from Annenberg Public Policy Center at the University of Pennsylvania: http://www.annenbergpublicpolicycenter.org/Downloads/Information_And_Society/TurowShoppingRelease.pdf

Baye, M. R., Gatti, J. R. J., Kattuman, P. & Morgan, J. (2007). A dashboard for online pricing. *California Management Review 50*(1), 202–216.

Dietz, K. (2008). *How to outpace the industry in snack sales and profit growth.* Retrieved December 28, 2011, from National Association of Convenience Stores: http://www.nacsonline.com/NACS/Resources/NACS%20Show%20Handouts/2008/How%20to%20Outpace%20the%20Industry%20in%20Snack%20Sales%20and%20Profit%20Growth.pdf

D'Innocenzio, A. (2012). J.C. Penney gets rids of hundreds of sales. Retrieved March 13, 2012, from Yahoo Finance: http://finance.yahoo.com/news/j-c-penney-gets-rid-151954852.html

Economides, N. (2012). Tying, bundling, and loyalty/requirement rebates. In: Einer Elhauge (Ed.), *Research handbook of the economics of antitrust law.* Edward Elgar Publishing: 121–143.

Elgin, B. (2004). *Google: Whiz kids or naughty boys?* Retrieved January 4, 2012, from Business Week: http://www.businessweek.com/technology/content/aug2004/tc20040819_6843_tc120.htm

Evers, J. (2006). *Microsoft's antivirus package makes a splash.* Retrieved January 18, 2012, from CNET: http://news.cnet.com/Microsofts-antivirus-package-makes-a-splash/2100-7355_3-6104926.html?tag=lia;rcol

Gil, R., & Hartmann, W. (2009). Empirical analysis of metering price discrimination: Evidence from concession sales at movie theaters. *Marketing Science 28*(6), 1046–1062.

Gregorowicz, P., & Hegji, C. (1998). Economics in the MBA curriculum: Some preliminary survey results. *Journal of Economic Education 29*(1), 81–87.

Kahneman, D. Knetsch, J.L., & Thaler, R. (1986). Fairness as a constraint on profit-seeking: Entitlements in the market. *American Economic Review 76*(4), 728–741.

Keeley, Kuenn, & Reid Law Firm. (2004). *What every business should know about price discrimination.* Retrieved January 2, 2012, from Keeley, Kuenn, and Reid Law Firm: http://www.kkrlaw.com/articles/kkr_price_discrimination_2004.pdf

Kolay, S., & Shaffer, G. (2003). Bundling and menus of two-part tariffs. *Journal of Industrial Economics 51*(3), 383–403.

Levy, S. (2009). *Secret of Googlenomics: Data-fueled recipe brews profitability.* Retrieved January 6, 2012, from Wired Magazine: http://www.wired.com/culture/culturereviews/magazine/17-06/nep_googlenomics?currentPage=all

Litman, T. (2011). *London congestion pricing: Implications for other cities.* Victoria, Canada: Victoria Transport Policy Institute.

Marburger, D. R. (2011). Re-designing managerial economics to suit the MBA. *International Journal of Pluralism and Economics Education 2*(2), 196–205.

Marden, O. S. (2011). The pioneer of marketing. Retrieved January 2, 2012, from The Ludwig Von Mises Institute: http://mises.org/daily/5054/The-Pioneer-of-Marketing

McAfee, R., & McMillan, J. (1987). Auctions and bidding. *Journal of Economic Literature 25*(2), 699–738.

Netessine, S., & Shumsky, R. (2002). Introduction to the theory and practice of yield management. *Informs Transactions on Education 3*(1), 34–44.

Oswald, E. (2011). *Netflix to raise monthly prices by as much as 60%.* Retrieved September 30, 2011, from PC World: http://www.pcworld.com/article/235556/netflix_to_raise_monthly_prices_by_as_much_as_60_percent.html

Otter, J. (2012). *Can J.C. Penney succeed like target and apple?* Retrieved March 13, 2012, from CBS News: http://www.cbsnews.com/8301-505268_162-57366649/can-j.c-penney-succeed-like-target-and-apple/

Ramasastry, A. (2005). Web sites change prices based on customers' habits. Retrieved January 4, 2012, from CNN.com: http://edition.cnn.com/2005/LAW/06/24/ramasastry.website.prices

Ross, T. (1984). Winners and losers under the Robinson–Patman Act. *Journal of Law and Economics 27*(2), 243–271.

Sahay, A. (2007). Now to reap higher profits with dynamic pricing. *MIT Sloan Management Review 48*(4), 53–60.

Slattery, B. (2010). *Netflix streaming-only plan arrives with price hike.* Retrieved September 30, 2011, from PC World: http://www.pcworld.com/article/211321/netflix_streamingonly_plan_arrives_with_price_hike.html

Stecklow, S. (1996). Colleges manipulate financial aid offers, shortchanging many. *Wall Street Journal,* April 1, 1996, A1.

Trumbull, M. (2011). *Netflix (NFLX) faces consumer backlash, weak economy.* Retrieved September 30, 2011, from The Christian Science Monitor: http://www.csmonitor.com/Business/2011/0919/Netflix-NFLX-faces-customer-backlash-weak-economy

Tully, S. (2000). Going, Going, Gone! The B2B tool that really is changing the world. Retrieved January 5, 2012, from CNN.com: http://money.cnn.com/magazines/fortune/fortune_archive/2000/03/20/276391/index.htm

U.S. Food and Drug Administration. (2009). *Facts and myths about generic drugs*. Retrieved March 13, 2012, from the U.S. Food and Drug Administration: http://www.fda.gov/Drugs/ResourcesForYou/Consumers/BuyingUsingMedicineSafely/UnderstandingGenericDrugs/ucm167991.htm

Vickrey, W. (1961). Counterspeculation, auctions, and competitive sealed tenders. *Journal of Finance 16*(1), 8–37.

Wald, M.L. (1998). So, how much did you pay for your ticket? *New York Times*, April, 12, 1998, 2.

Waldner, G. (2011). *How colleges discriminate with price and why they must stop*. Retrieved February 9, 2012, from Forbes.com: http://www.forbes.com/2011/06/10/college-price-tuition-discrimination.html

Weiss, R. M., & Mehrotra, A.K. (2001). Online dynamic pricing: Efficiency, equity, and the future of e-commerce. *Virginia Journal of Law and Technology 6*(2), 1–11.

Welsh, J. (2011). Hybrid sales surge as gas prices march upward. Retrieved December 31, 2011, from Wall Street Journal: http://blogs.wsj.com/drivers-seat/2011/04/06/hybrid-sales-surge-as-gas-prices-march-upward

Zuckerman, L. (1998). Musical fares. Same plan, same destination, same seats. So why does one cost $220, the other $1142? *New York Times Magazine*, March 8, 73.

Index

Announcing the Business Expert Press Digital Library

Concise E-books Business Students Need for Classroom and Research

This book can also be purchased in an e-book collection by your library as

- a one-time purchase,
- that is owned forever,
- allows for simultaneous readers,
- has no restrictions on printing, and
- can be downloaded as PDFs from within the library community.

Our digital library collections are a great solution to beat the rising cost of textbooks. e-books can be loaded into their course management systems or onto student's e-book readers.

The **Business Expert Press** digital libraries are very affordable, with no obligation to buy in future years. For more information, please visit **www.businessexpertpress.com/librarians**. To set up a trial in the United States, please contact **Adam Chesler** at *adam.chesler@businessexpertpress. com* for all other regions, contact **Nicole Lee** at *nicole.lee@igroupnet.com.*

OTHER TITLES IN OUR ECONOMICS AND FINANCE COLLECTION

Collection Editors: **Philip Romero and Jeffrey A. Edwards**

- *Managerial Economics Concepts and Principles* by Donald Stengel
- *Your Macroeconomic Edge Investing Strategies for the Post-Recession World* by Donald Philip J. Romero
- *Working with Economic Indicators Interpretation and Sources* by Donald Stengel

CPSIA information can be obtained at www.ICGtesting.com
Printed in the USA
BVOW042343200812

298268BV00004B/4/P